Alif Baa

مدخل الى حروف العربية وأصواتها

Introduction to Arabic Letters and Sounds

كرستن بروستاد Kristen Brustad

محمود البطل Mahmoud Al-Batal

عباس التونسي Abbas Al-Tonsi

Georgetown University Press
Washington, DC

Third Edition - الطبعة الثالثة

The production of the first edition of this textbook was supported by a grant from the National Endowment for the Humanities, an independent federal agency.

Library of Congress Cataloging-in-Publication Data

Brustad, Kristen.
   Alif baa : introduction to Arabic letters and sounds / Kristen Brustad, Mahmoud Al-Batal, Abbas Al-Tonsi. -- 3rd ed.
      p. cm.
   In English and Arabic.
   Includes bibliographical references and index.
   ISBN 978-1-58901-632-3 (pbk. : alk. paper) -- ISBN 978-1-58901-644-6 (cloth)
   1. Arabic language--Writing. 2. Arabic alphabet. I. Al-Batal, Mahmoud. II. Tunisi, Abbas. III. Title.
   PJ6123.B78 2010
   492.78--dc22   2009024933

DVD ISBN 978-1-58901-633-0
∞ This book is printed on acid-free paper meeting the requirements of the American National Standard for Permanence in Paper for Printed Library Materials.

19 18 17   10 9 8

Printed in the United States of America

Contents

Unit Four الوحدة الرابعة

Unit Five الوحدة الخامسة

Preface to the Student

Ahlan wa Sahlan! Welcome to Arabic! This textbook, *Alif Baa*, represents the first in a series of textbooks aimed at teaching Arabic to English-speaking students, followed by *Al-Kitaab fii Taʿallum al-ʿArabiyya I, II,* and *III.* The present book aims to help you learn to pronounce the sounds of Arabic and write its letters, and to begin speaking Arabic. Unit 1 will give you an overview of Arabic, and units 2 through 10 will introduce you to the letters, sounds, and symbols that make up the Arabic writing system. In addition to the sounds and letters of Arabic, *Alif Baa* will introduce and help you master over two hundred words of basic vocabulary, including important expressions for polite interaction with speakers of Arabic.

The materials are designed for you to prepare at home and come to class ready to speak, read, and write using what you have studied outside class. Everyone learns at his or her own pace, and class time is limited, so it will be much more efficient for you to prepare the material, listen, and practice at your own speed. The textbook and accompanying media are designed to give you everything you need to study and learn the sounds, letters, and vocabulary.

Alif Baa is accompanied by audio, video, and interactive exercises available on a companion website, www.alkitaabtextbook.com, to be used outside of class. We have designed the book to work best with the companion website, and we encourage you and your teachers to use it. Each book also includes a DVD with the same audio and video that is on the website and everything that is needed to complete all of the exercises, in case you do not have reliable internet access. You know to turn to the DVD or website when you see the 🎧. The website can be used by independent learners or by a class, as most of the exercises are instantly graded for immediate feedback.

In addition to audio and video exercises and activities, you will watch a calligrapher write the letters so that you have a model to follow as you work through them. The materials also contain some print examples of authentic or "real-life" Arabic from various sources, and we have included short cultural notes that explain some aspects of the situations that you will see in the scenes. You will find English–Arabic and Arabic–English glossaries at the end of the book that include all the words and expressions introduced in the book as active vocabulary. Please read the introductions to the glossaries before using them because each glossary is designed for specific purposes.

All of the listening and writing exercises in *Alif Baa* are designed as homework for you to do in preparation for class. This approach allows you to study and learn at your own pace and saves class time for interactive activities. A feature that is new in this third edition of the program are a number of interactive, autocorrecting exercises on the interactive media that give you immediate feedback. It is very important that you work through all of these exercises as thoroughly as you can, and that you tell your instructor if you are having trouble with them in the form of many missed answers, or if you feel that you are just guessing and not answering. Your instructor should collect from you and check the dictation and letter-connection exercises to check on your progress. In this edition the dictation exercises are recorded in video rather than audio so that you can take advantage of the visual clues to help you hear and write the words correctly.

We believe that it is crucial for you to learn to recognize and produce Arabic sounds accurately from the outset for several reasons. First, you must learn to pronounce Arabic correctly in order to communicate effectively with Arabic speakers. Second, Arabic sounds are not very difficult. Many nonnative speakers have learned to pronounce Arabic sounds accurately as adults, and you should expect to do so as well. Third, it is important to learn the sounds correctly now when you have the time to concentrate on them; later you will be concentrating on other aspects of the language, such as vocabulary and grammar. Fourth, the Arabic language is structured around groups of consonant sounds that carry meaning, so the ability to recognize sounds accurately when you hear them will greatly enhance your ability to understand, learn, and remember vocabulary. Fifth, Arabic is largely phonetic, which means that if you learn the sounds correctly now, you will not suffer from spelling headaches later.

These materials include three different varieties of Arabic: The spoken Arabic of Cairo, the spoken Arabic of Damascus, and formal Arabic. Your instructor will decide which form or forms he or she wants you to activate, or learn to produce. You may want to listen to other varieties for exposure. You will notice that much of the vocabulary is shared but that some words differ from one variety or another. The key to dealing with the richness of variation in Arabic is to differentiate between what you recognize and what you use actively. Choose one form to use actively and leave the others for recognition. This is what native speakers do when they interact with people from other countries, and it is an important skill to develop.

We hope that the following principles will help you use these materials as they were designed to be used:

(1) Study actively and interactively. Studying actively means that you are producing something, whether you are repeating sounds and words out loud, writing words, or creating sentences. Practice speaking every chance you get, with classmates, the dog, or to yourself. Most successful language learners talk out loud to themselves regularly. Study with a classmate because you are much more likely to study actively when you study with a partner. Every lesson in this book contains activities that are best done in pairs. The book and materials give you several open-ended exercises that you can do more than once, each time differently. Prepare for active participation in class too: Anticipate what you will be doing and be ready by planning and rehearsing the things you can say and do beforehand.

(2) Be an audiovisual learner. Although most of your studies now are visually oriented, you learned your native language mainly through hearing and listening rather than through reading and writing. As children, most of us watched films and television programs and had the same stories read to us over and over, and this repetition helped us to learn our native language. Each time you watch and listen you can learn something new, whether it is the way a vowel sounds with this new consonant or the way words are put together in a new sentence. As adult learners we can speed up this process with visual material as well, but the more you can integrate sound and shape and associate the two together, the faster your progress to fluency in Arabic will proceed. Engage more than one faculty at the same time: Repeat aloud while you are listening, and rather than write silently, say and repeat whatever you are writing out loud.

(3) Once is not enough. Listen to the audio and video material and practice writing the letters many times. Whether you are pronouncing new sounds, writing new letters, or studying vocabulary, you should repeat the activity until you can produce the sound or word comfortably and be able to "hear" it in your mind or write it in a shape that you are pleased with. Remember that you are training your brain and your muscles to do new things, and this takes practice.

(4) Own it. Make the words you are learning relevant to your life by using them to talk about your world. Personalizing vocabulary is the fastest way to memorize it. Own the sounds too: Once you learn them, they are not foreign sounds, they belong to you.

(5) Make the review and study of vocabulary part of your day. Language is cumulative, and while you are learning new words and expressions, it is important to integrate them with previously learned material. Pair up each new word with an old one. Using the new to review the old will take some organization, but it will pay off in greater fluency and accuracy. When you learn new words, take the opportunity to work on previously learned sounds. When you learn new letters, go back to old vocabulary to see if you can write any of them in Arabic script.

(6) Learning a language is a lot like learning to play a sport. The idea is to have fun while building skills. Both entail lots of repetition and exercises that build mental and physical strength. Expect to feel tired occasionally. Being tired is a good sign—it means that you are concentrating and learning actively.

Learning language requires exposure, time, and effort. The single most important factor in your success is your belief in your ability to learn Arabic. We wish you a successful and enjoyable learning experience!

Teacher's Guide

This textbook, and the continuing books in the *Al-Kitaab* program, are constructed around a philosophy of teaching and learning Arabic that continues to evolve. We ask that you, the instructor, read the Preface to the Student before reading this guide, that you have your students read it at home, and then discuss it with them in class so everyone understands the approach underlying the structure and contents of these materials.

It is crucial that you read through this entire book *before* teaching it so you can formulate your own vision of what the students can learn by the time they finish: What they will be able to read, write, and most importantly, say. This vision will affect the way you teach these materials. You also need to be well acquainted with the interactive materials that accompany this textbook, precisely because the students will be using them outside of class more than in class. Students will take their cue from you, the instructor, in the importance they attach to working with these materials and the way they approach them. The book is designed to work best with the companion website, www.alkitaabtextbook.com, which provides instant feedback to the at-home exercises that the students will complete. If either you or your students do not have reliable internet access, a DVD is included that contains all of the same audio and video material that is included on the website. We encourage you to become familiar with all of the features of the website before you begin to teach.

Alif Baa consists of ten units and English–Arabic and Arabic–English glossaries. Unit 1 provides an overview of Arabic, including the transliteration system that is used to introduce vocabulary that cannot yet be written in Arabic. In this third edition of *Alif Baa*, the transliteration system has increased importance because of our decision to introduce vocabulary according to its functionality, not spelling; that is, many words are introduced to the students to be actively learned before they can write them in Arabic. Units 2 through 8 present the alphabet in groups that follow the modern Arabic order, with the exception that و and ي are presented in unit 2. Each unit contains a number of recorded listening exercises and drills on the alphabet and sound system, including reading, writing, connecting letters, and dictation. Students should complete all of the listening exercises and writing practice exercises at home. In this edition many of the listening drills have been transformed into interactive, autocorrecting exercises that the students will also do at home. This will result in less correcting for the instructor but will increase the importance of the correcting you will do to make sure satisfactory progress is being made.

In describing the sounds, we have avoided technical descriptions, opting instead for a more practical approach that uses tips and exercises that focus on the points of articulation of the sounds. Following the description of each sound, we have provided a brief explanation about the writing of the corresponding letter that is meant to accompany the video showing calligrapher Sayyid El-Shinnawi drawing each of the letters. Please encourage students to watch these video portions as they work through the book. The materials are designed so that you do not have to waste time explaining the sounds and letters in class. Students should prepare at home and be ready to read and write in class.

Materials in *Alif Baa* integrate formal and spoken registers of Arabic and lay the foundation for the approach that is used throughout the *Al-Kitaab* series. This third edition of *Alif Baa* differs from the second edition in several important ways. You will notice the addition of Levantine Arabic scenes, filmed in Damascus, that run parallel to the Egyptian scenes. A more important change, however, is the way in which the colloquial materials have been incorporated into the pedagogy. In this edition spoken forms of vocabulary are presented alongside formal Arabic forms in writing, and vocabulary lists give students the option of learning a set of words in formal Arabic, Egyptian, or Levantine. In addition, many of the vocabulary exercises and activities include colloquial words and expressions, and students are given opportunities to practice and activate these forms. We believe that you will be pleased with what your students can do with Arabic by using just a few colloquial expressions and having the freedom to create with the language.

Alif Baa, third edition, gives you, the instructor, more choices. In addition to the letters and sounds, each unit contains vocabulary and dialogues designed to be prepared at home and activated in class. The vocabulary is introduced in formal Arabic as well as in two dialects, and you must choose which of these varieties you will ask students to activate. Our experience working with multiple varieties in class has demonstrated to us that students have no trouble being exposed to more than one variety of Arabic, as long as they are not held responsible for "purity"—that is, as long as you allow them flexibility to decide which form they want to use.

The main philosophical principles that underlie the design of these materials can be summarized as follows:

(1) Arabic is one language, rich in registers and varieties.
Each register of Arabic reflects vital parts of Arab culture, so students need to learn formal and informal varieties to understand the language and the culture. Our decision to include an introduction to colloquial Arabic is also a natural consequence of our desire to use language forms that are appropriate to context. A basic colloquial vocabulary of approximately twenty-five words out of approximately two hundred presented in this book gives learners the tools they need to begin to express and communicate with native speakers in their immediate environment who will not speak to them in formal Arabic. In this third edition you and your students have new Syrian versions of the colloquial dialogues so you can have a choice of which dialect to teach. We have included formal Arabic vocabulary for those who prefer to work in this register, but we have not recorded dialogues in formal Arabic because of its artificiality in such contexts. This is not the time to worry about the mixing of registers in speech or in writing. Students' ability to choose appropriate vocabulary for the situation or context will evolve over time. The three crucial speaking skills to develop at this stage are pronunciation of sounds, gender agreement, and correct use (conjugation in context) of the forms of the verb we have included here.

(2) Everyone can produce Arabic sounds accurately, and it is necessary to encourage and to expect accuracy from the outset.
Not only is this an excellent opportunity for you and your students to focus all of your attention on the phonetic aspects of Arabic, it is also better to form good habits from the start. We believe that all language skills are important and that they reinforce each other. The

ability to hear the difference between, for example, ك and ق is a necessary prelude to being able to produce them, and the ability to do both will aid in mastering Arabic morphology, the root and pattern system, spelling, and retaining vocabulary. Your attitude as a teacher of Arabic should be that everyone can learn to produce these sounds.

(3) It is crucial to set high expectations while maintaining an encouraging and cooperative atmosphere in class by rewarding success verbally and often.

It is our job to expect a high degree of effort from students in preparing for class, and to reward this effort by spending class time doing interactive and small-group activities that permit maximum participation from all students. The book is designed so that the students can do much of their learning outside of class, each person working at his or her own pace so differences in learning speed will not affect the class as a whole. It is also important that students realize right away that the burden of learning is on them, because this helps them to become active learners. Finally, it is essential to follow through on the expectations you set. By "teaching" them what they should have done outside of class, you might inadvertently reward students who have not prepared and punish those who have.

(4) Vocabulary is the foundation of Arabic skills.

Grammar is necessary but not difficult; more important, the grammar that a student needs at the Novice level is simple and can be activated along with vocabulary. A major shift in this edition with regard to the treatment of vocabulary is our decision to introduce words and expressions in functional rather than alphabetical order; that is, words are introduced when they can be productively used, not when they can be written in Arabic script. Please note that the vocabulary used in listening and handwriting exercises *is not active* vocabulary. The meanings of some of these words are given merely as entertainment, so the learner knows that he or she is writing meaningful words. We have used only meaningful words throughout these materials because word structure in Arabic is based on consonant–vowel patterns, and we believe that listening to a large number of words, even if one does not know their meaning, will help learners begin to internalize these patterns and facilitate learning vocabulary. Active vocabulary is introduced in the vocabulary charts and recorded for students to listen to and learn at home.

(5) The multiple varieties and registers of Arabic constitute a richness to be embraced, not feared.

Our decision to introduce vocabulary in spoken and formal Arabic may blur the boundaries between these two registers; however, the reality of Arabic today is that these boundaries are quite porous. Even in the most formal of contexts, spoken forms of Arabic are often heard mixed in with formal Arabic. Moreover, most Arabic-speaking populations living in communities outside the Arab world, or in the Gulf, are exposed to and interact with dialects different from their own on a regular basis, and in such multidialect situations, few speakers maintain "pure" dialect. We do not need to expect a level of "purity" from our students that does not exist in the community or in the world around them. If your students will interact with Palestinians, Lebanese, Egyptians, or Moroccans outside of class, they will be exposed to different words. We can embrace this variety and richness of Arabic. Students' attitudes toward Arabic may reflect your own, so think carefully about what you project to them.

Designing your syllabus

We believe that this material can be actively learned in approximately twenty-two class hours plus forty-four to fifty homework hours, including quizzes and a skit presentation. Students should be told from the outset to expect two hours of homework for every hour in class. We suggest the following schedule as a rule of thumb in planning your syllabus.

Unit	Class Hours	Homework Hours
1	1	2
2	2	4
3	2	4-5
4	3	6-7
5	3	6-7
6	3	6-7
7	3	6-7
8	2	4-5
9	2	4
10	1	2
Total	**22**	**44-50**

Notice that units 4, 5, and 6 are longer than other units, in part because of the extra work needed on emphatic letters and sounds. Because of their length, these lessons have been constructed with two different sets of vocabulary and speaking work so that a balance of alphabet and speaking work can be maintained day-to-day. An extra class hour is built into unit 7 because of the large number of activities in it. This time projection rests on several key assumptions:

(1) The purpose of a textbook is to present information to the learner for acquisition outside of class, and the purpose of class time is to activate (not present or explain) the material that students have prepared at home. These materials have been designed so that students can do most of the preparation and studying of new material outside of class in order for class time to be spent doing interactive activities, practicing writing in the form of in-class dictation exercises, and practicing conversations. Assign all of the listening and writing exercises as homework so that students learn the sounds and letters at their own pace at home. In class, have them activate what they have studied through dictation practice of your own design and in-class exercises. As a new feature in this edition, the vocabulary lists include all of the expressions in the colloquial dialogues and allow students to prepare everything, even the dialogues, at home before coming to class. This approach has several important pedagogical benefits.

First, it allows students to work at their own pace and avoids the frustration that can be experienced by students of different backgrounds and abilities. Second, the steps that we have provided in these exercises will help students develop listening strategies and encourage them to think not just about what they are listening to but how they are listening. These are strategies that you can encourage and build upon in class as well. Third, it allows more class time for activation: Rather than spending half an hour listening (passively) to the dialogue, students can come to class prepared to discuss what they saw and heard with a partner, listen one more time in preparation for activation, and spend at least twenty minutes in conversation with their classmates, moving from one partner to another for variety.

(2) Class time should be distributed between two types of activities: sound and letter work in the form of dictation and paired reading exercises, and conversation and vocabulary practice in pairs and small groups. The distribution formula will depend on your goals and

priorities. If you believe speaking skills are important, we suggest that you aim to have at least some interactive work during every class period, and that the time set aside for this activity increase as students learn more vocabulary so that by the time you reach the end of the book, you are spending 65% to 75% of class time with students working together speaking directly with each other. Working in pairs and small groups is essential for students to build language skills and confidence. While it is true that the instructor may sacrifice a degree of control in this kind of classroom, the success of this approach in building speaking skills is clear. You will not be able to correct every utterance, but accuracy will improve if students see it rewarded. In the end, it is self-correction, not teacher correction, that underlies accurate speaking. Our goal is to train students to correct themselves and help each other, and our challenge is to create an atmosphere that demands accuracy in pronunciation with encouragement to create freely. We believe that it is good policy to reassure students that they will never be penalized for trying to say something new using the words they are learning.

(3) Homework should be corrected as it is prepared, that is, outside of class. Many of the exercises autocorrect on the interactive media, which has the advantage of giving students immediate feedback. However, the fact that you will not see this work makes it all the more important that you collect and go over the dictation and letter-connection drills to make sure that the students are making good progress. Students should devote around two hours a night to homework and class preparation. All of the listening exercises in the textbook are meant to be done at home, and the drills are all labeled *At home, In class*, or both.

(4) Our approach stresses dictation because we believe that the mastery of sounds and the ability to relate sounds and writing must be developed early. For in-class dictation, use your own words rather than those in the book or on the homework. In the beginning you will want to repeat words many times and have students repeat as a group to take the pressure off individual performance. It takes several repetitions of a new or unfamiliar sound in order to identify it, and several more to be able to produce it. Later, as students' skills develop, you may want to limit your repetitions to three to five times to help students develop their "active memory" listening skills. It is very important to give students feedback on their dictation skills during the activity. If you can have some or all the students write on the board, you can check their progress most easily. It is also beneficial, if possible, to have an assistant in class who can go around the room and help students individually during dictation time. An advanced nonnative student can fill this role if your program allows it, and it is encouraging for beginning students to see nonnative peers who are successful learners of Arabic.

(5) Active learning of vocabulary is the single biggest challenge that faces the learner of Arabic. Native speakers of Arabic start their study of Arabic in school already knowing six years' worth of vocabulary; the foreign learner has none and needs to catch up before mastering the intricacies of formal Arabic syntax. In the forthcoming third editions of the other books in the *Al-Kitaab* textbook program, there will be increases in the amount of vocabulary and exercises, and this new edition of *Alif Baa* is no exception. Each unit includes at least one vocabulary section and several exercises and activities for activation, most of which are designed to be prepared at home and activated in class. You will also find interactive vocabulary activities with phrases and sentences. By unit 6 you can push the students to

produce sentences (not just words), and we expect the students to have reached between Novice Mid and Novice High proficiency by the time they finish these materials. The key to this achievement is time spent activating vocabulary in context.

Of course, no textbook can take the place of a good teacher. It is our hope that these materials will help you to enrich your classroom and make learning Arabic an enjoyable and productive experience for your students.

مع أطيب تمنياتنا لكم بالتوفيق

Acknowledgments

Arabic calligraphy by Professor Sayyid El-Shinnawi, Zayid University, U.A.E.

Production of Egyptian colloquial video materials by Nashwa Mohsin Zayid, Cairo, Egypt.

Production of Syrian colloquial video materials by Maya Patsalides, Direct Line Media Production, Damascus, Syria.

Design and composition of the book by ObjectDC, Vienna, Virginia.

Illustrations by Lucinda Levine, Chevy Chase, Maryland.

This third edition of *Alif Baa* builds upon the work of many talented and dedicated people who also contributed to the first and second editions, and it would not have been possible without their enthusiastic participation. The National Endowment for the Humanities provided the funding for the first edition of the textbook through a grant to the School of Arabic at Middlebury College, and Middlebury College provided matching funds and staff support for this project. The Emory College Language Center and its staff, Jose Rodriguez, Johnny Waggener, and student assistant Khaled Krisht, provided invaluable technical assistance during all phases of producing the second edition. We are grateful to Mohammad Shaheen and his talented and dedicated team in Egypt who patiently worked and reworked everything from sounds to the screen fonts to produce the best-quality DVDs possible at the time we produced the second edition. The creativity of previous editions' artists Anne Marie Skye and Michael Cooperson is acknowledged with gratitude.

The quality of audiovisual contributions in the previous editions are evident in their continued role in this new edition. We are indebted to Sayyid El-Shinnawi for his beautiful calligraphy, which makes a big difference not only in the aesthetic quality of the new edition but also in its educational value. *Alf shukr* to our colleagues Housni Bennis, Ikram Masmoudi, Olla Al-Shalchi, Awad Mubarak, Shukri Gohar, and Wafa Abouneaj for their beautiful video introductions. Among our former students who contributed to the project, we would like to mention in particular Adriana Valencia and Melanie Clouser, whose contributions to previous glossaries remain present here. We are also grateful to Rima Semaan and Khaled Krisht for lending their beautiful voices and pronunciation models to the audio materials.

A special acknowledgment is also due to our video producers, Nashwa Mohsin Zayid and Maya Patsalides, and to the cinematography teams they assembled. The directors, actors, and camera and sound professionals worked extremely long hours to create the colloquial dialogue scenes in the accompanying interactive component. The extra effort they put into filming and editing have resulted in the fine product you now have. We are very grateful to Iman Fandi for creating the Syrian version of the *Alif Baa* dialogues and for working with Ms. Patsalides to film them.

The Department of Middle Eastern Studies at the University of Texas has not only been a supportive academic home for Mahmoud Al-Batal and Kristen Brustad, but has also provided the opportunity to develop the pedagogy in new directions. The superb audio and video engineers at Liberal Arts Instructional Technology Services, Daniel Garza, Mike Heidenreich, and Kevin West, provided outstanding audio and video recording services for the project. We are grateful to our UT colleagues, including our junior colleagues, the graduate student instructors, for the inspiring atmosphere created by their energy and commitment. The first-year Arabic team of fall 2008, including Martha Schulte-Nafeh, who continues to offer valuable suggestions and comments to the *Al-Kitaab* textbook program; Dina H. Mostafa, Kevin Burnham, Summer Loomis, Cory Jorgenson, Steve Robertson, Drew Paul, and Nasser al-Maamari, enthusiastically participated in piloting many of the new ideas introduced here. Steve Robertson contributed in important ways by translating the principle of integrating formal and spoken Arabic that has evolved further in this edition. A special thanks to Dina Mostafa and Charles Joukhadar for their contributions to the audio and video recordings of this edition, and to Nesrine Ourari and Nasser al-Maamari for their Tunisian and Omani dialect contributions.

Georgetown University's School of Foreign Service in Qatar has provided Abbas Al-Tonsi with both the opportunity to teach the *Al-Kitaab* textbook program and the supportive collegial environment that made collecting and developing new materials possible. Our colleagues at Georgetown University Press were instrumental in helping us realize the ambitious additions to this third edition of *Alif Baa*. Special thanks go to the entire Georgetown University Press staff, but in particular to Richard Brown, director; Gail Grella, senior acquisitions editor; and Hope LeGro, director of Georgetown Languages, for the many necessary contributions to bring this new and improved edition to fruition.

Last but not least, we thank all the students and colleagues who have used the previous editions of the book and who took the trouble to write us with suggestions for improvements. We have incorporated as many as possible, and we hope that the new edition will continue to serve the needs of its users.

مع خالص الشكر والتقدير لكم جميعاً

الوحدة الأولى
Unit One

In this unit:

The Arabic Alphabet

Special Characteristics of Arabic Script

Pronunciation of Arabic

Formal and Spoken Arabic

A Transliteration System

Vocabulary and Conversation:
Greetings and Introductions

New Vocabulary

Egyptian and Levantine Colloquial

Video Dialogues

Culture: Saying Hello

>> Letters and Sounds

The Arabic Alphabet

The Arabic alphabet contains twenty-eight letters, including consonants and long vowels, and fourteen symbols that function as short vowels and pronunciation markers, or as markers of certain grammatical functions. Units 2 through 10 introduce these letters and symbols individually. You will work with the workbook and the interactive media in tandem, and in the text you will see this media symbol , which indicates that you should listen to or watch the interactive media. The chart below shows the twenty-eight letters. Starting in the upper right-hand corner, the chart reads across from right to left, which is the direction Arabic is written and read.

Listening Exercise 1. Arabic letters and sounds (At home)

Watch the videos to see and hear the pronunciation of these letters.

The next chart shows the fourteen extra-alphabetical symbols and their names. They include short vowels, pronunciation symbols, grammatical endings, spelling variants, and a consonant that, for historical reasons, is not represented in the alphabet chart. These symbols will be introduced in units 2 through 10 along with the alphabet.

ِ kasra	ُ Damma	َ fatHa
ٍ tanwiin al-kasr	ٌ tanwiin aD-Damm	ً tanwiin al-fatH
أ waSla	ّ shadda	ْ Sukuun
ا dagger alif	آ alif madda	ى alif maqSuura
	ء hamza	ة taa marbuuTa

Special Characteristics of Arabic Script

The Arabic alphabet and writing system has four major characteristics that distinguish it from its European counterparts.

(1) Arabic is written from right to left. One consequence of this directionality is that Arabic books, newspapers, and magazines are opened and read in the opposite direction from European and American printed materials.

(2) Letters are connected in both print and script, unlike those of the Latin alphabet, which are connected only in script. The following individual letters are written one after the other. However, even though these letters occur in the correct combination and order, they do not form a word when they are written this way: ا ل ب ا ب When they are connected, however, they do spell a word: الباب (al-baab *the door*).

Notice that not all the letters in الباب connect to the following letter. This is a characteristic of certain letters that you will master as you learn to write. See if you can identify the nonconnecting letters in the following words:

مبارك   أسد   زين   السودان   لذيذ

As you learn the alphabet, note which letters connect and which do not. When you write words, it is important not to lift the pen or pencil from the page until you get to a natural break at a nonconnecting letter.

(3) Letters have slightly different shapes depending on where they occur in a word. The alphabet chart at the beginning of this unit gives the forms of the letters when they are written independently; however, these forms vary when the letters are written in initial, medial, or final position. "Initial position" means that the letter is not connected to a previous letter. "Medial position" indicates that the letter is between two other letters.

"Final position" means that the letter is connected to the preceding letter. Most letters have a particularly distinct shape when they occur in the final position, similar to the way English uses initial uppercase letters for words that begin sentences.

The chart below gives you an idea of the extent of this variation. You will see that each letter retains a basic shape throughout, which is the core of the letter. If the letter has a dot, the number and position also remain the same. Note that the last three letters, which all connect, appear to have a "tail" in their independent and final forms that drops off when they are connected and is replaced by a connecting segment that rests on the line. Look for the core shape of each letter; its dots, if any; the connecting segments; and the final tail in the following chart.

Final position	Medial position	Initial position	Independent shape
ـا	ـا	ا	ا
ـث	ـثـ	ثـ	ث
ـج	ـجـ	جـ	ج
ـع	ـعـ	عـ	ع

[handwritten note in margin: se convierte así porque se hace más fácil de conectar a otras letras]

As you learn each letter of the alphabet you will learn to read and write all of its various shapes. You will be surprised how quickly you master them with a little practice! (4) Arabic script consists of two separate "layers" of writing. The basic skeleton of a word is made up of the consonants and long vowels. Short vowels and other pronunciation and grammatical markers are separated from the consonant skeleton of the word. This second layer, called *vocalization* or *vowelling*, is normally omitted in writing, and the reader recognizes words without it. Compare the following two versions of the same text, a line of poetry, the first of which represents the normal way of writing without vocalization, and the second of which has all the pronunciation markers added:

بسقط اللوى بين الدخول فحومل   قفا نبك من ذكرى حبيب ومنزل

بِسِقْطِ ٱللِّوى بَيْنَ ٱلدَّخُولِ فَحَوْمَلِ   قِفا نَبْكِ مِنْ ذِكْرى حَبِيبٍ وَمَنْزِلِ

من معلقة امرئ القيس (The Great Qays)

Texts that are normally vocalized include elementary school textbooks, some editions of classical literary texts, and religious texts such as the Qur'an and the Bible. In scripture this precision has religious significance: The extra markings on the text leave no doubt as to the exact reading intended. Thus the texts of the Qur'an and Bible show full vocalization, as you can see in the following excerpts.

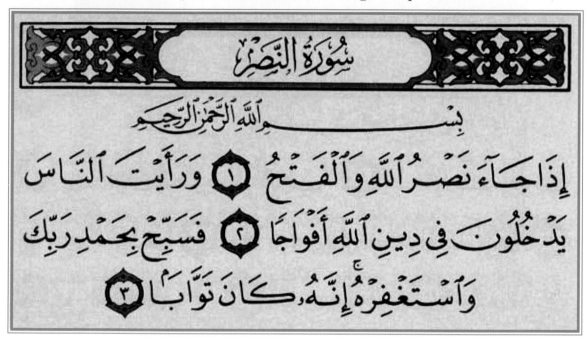

سورة النصر من القرآن الكريم

سِفْرُ التَّكْوِينِ: الْأَصْحَاحُ الْأَوَّلُ

١فِي الْبَدْءِ خَلَقَ اللّهُ السَّمَاوَاتِ وَالْأَرْضَ

٢وَكَانَتِ الْأَرْضُ خَرِبَةً وَخَالِيَةً، وَعَلَى وَجْهِ الْغَمْرِ ظُلْمَةٌ، وَرُوحُ اللّهِ

يَرِفُّ عَلَى وَجْهِ الْمِيَاهِ ٣وَقَالَ اللّهُ: "لِيَكُنْ نُورٌ"، فَكَانَ نُورٌ

٤وَرَأَى اللّهُ النُّورَ أَنَّهُ حَسَنٌ. وَفَصَلَ اللّهُ بَيْنَ النُّورِ وَالظُّلْمَةِ.

٥وَدَعَا اللّهُ النُّورَ نَهَارًا، وَالظُّلْمَةُ دَعَاهَا لَيْلاً. وَكَانَ مَسَاءٌ وَكَانَ صَبَاحٌ يَوْمًا وَاحِدًا.

الخدمة العربية للكرازة بالإنجيل

In schoolbooks, vowel markings are used to introduce new vocabulary and to enable the students to learn the correct pronunciation of formal Arabic with all the correct grammatical endings. The following example is taken from an elementary reader used in Qatar.

كُلُّ شَعْبٍ لَهُ مَلابِسُ خاصَّةٌ بِهِ، تَخْتَلِفُ عَنْ مَلابِسِ الشُّعوبِ الأُخْرى قَلِيلاً أَوْ كَثيراً. وَالْمَلابِسُ عَلى اخْتِلافِ أَشْكالِها، تَحْفَظُ الْجِسْمَ مِنَ الأَذى، وَتَحْميهِ مِنَ الْحَرِّ وَالْبَرْدِ وَتُعْطيهِ مَنْظَراً جَميلاً

(اللغة العربية للصف الثاني الابتدائي، الفصل الدراسي الأول، وزارة التعليم بقطر ٢٠٠٨)

Once students learn the new words, they see them in regular, unvocalized script. You will learn vocabulary the same way. Most books, magazines, and newspapers are unvocalized, like the following newspaper article.

٦٩٣ ألفاً يفقدون وظائفهم في أمريكا

● نيويورك – رويترز – أفاد تقرير أعدته أمس شركة خاصة للتوظيف ، بأن القطاع الخاص فقد ٦٩٣ ألف وظيفة في كانون الأول (ديسمبر) الماضي ، مقارنة بـ ٤٧٦ ألفاً في تشرين الثاني (نوفمبر) وبمعدل يفوق تقديرات الخبراء الاقتصاديين بشدة.

وبلغ متوسط تقديرات ٢٠ خبيراً استطلعت وكالة "رويترز" توقعاتهم للتقرير الذي تصدره شركة "ايه دي بي" لخدمات أصحاب الأعمال، ٤٧٣ ألفاً.

من جريدة الحياة ٢٠٠٩/١/٨

In unvocalized texts, possible ambiguities in form arise every once in a while; however, the meaning is almost always clear from the context. In the rare cases in which there may be some ambiguity, a clarifying vowel may be added. In the *Al-Kitaab* textbook program, vocalization marks will be used when new vocabulary is introduced, but thereafter you will be expected to have memorized the pronunciation of the word, and these marks will be omitted. Since Arabic speakers normally read and write without vocalization, it is best to become accustomed to reading and writing that way from the beginning.

Pronunciation of Arabic

In addition to recognizing the characteristics of the Arabic script, you should also be aware of certain features about the sounds of Arabic.

(1) Arabic has a one-to-one correspondence between sound and letter, whereas English spelling often uses one letter or combination of letters to represent several different sounds. Consider the plural marker *s* in the words *dogs* and *books*, and note that the sound of the first is actually *z*, not *s*. Compare also the two different sounds spelled as *th* as in *think* and *those*. These are two distinct sounds, and Arabic has two different letters to represent them. American English speakers sometimes confuse pronunciation and spelling without realizing it. For example, think about the word *television*. This word has been adopted into Arabic and is pronounced something like *tilivizyoon*. It is also spelled with the Arabic letter that corresponds to the sound *z* because that is the way it is pronounced. English spelling, on the other hand, requires an *s*, even though there is no *s* sound in the word. The letters we use to write English can represent different sounds, so it is better to associate Arabic sounds not with individual letters but rather with words so you can remember which sound corresponds to the Arabic sound you are learning. For example, associate the sound *th* with *three*, and *s* with *so*. This will be particularly important when you learn Arabic vowel sounds.

(2) The Arabic writing system is regularly phonetic, which means that words are generally written the way they are pronounced. If you learn to recognize and pronounce the sounds correctly from the beginning, you will avoid spelling problems and you will learn and retain vocabulary more easily.

(3) In general, sounds in Arabic use a wider range of mouth and throat positions than do sounds in English. To properly produce these sounds, be aware of the parts of the mouth and throat you must use while you are able to focus the most attention on them. You will learn to make new sounds, and to do so you must become familiar with the set of muscles that you use to make sounds like gargling or coughing but not to speak English. Your muscles are capable of making all these sounds, but you need to become conscious of what they are doing and practice constantly in the beginning.

Like sports, learning a language takes physical work along with mental focus. Just as you train your arm through repeated practice to hit a tennis ball, you must train your mouth to produce new sounds and combinations of sounds, and this takes constant repetition. Just like you keep your eye on the ball in tennis, you must also keep your mind on the sounds you are making at all times. An investment of time and effort into developing your pronunciation habits during the first month of learning Arabic will pay off later in that you will be able to learn, pronounce, and spell vocabulary more easily; you will understand other people better; and people will also understand you, which in turn will encourage them to speak with you in Arabic rather than in English.

Formal and Spoken Arabic

Every language has different registers (levels of formality) and varieties (dialects) that vary according to speaker or writer and situation or function. For example, *I dunno* is rarely written, except for special effect, and *I do not know* is rarely used in speech. *Hoagie, submarine, sub, wedge*, and *hero* are names that all refer to the same sandwich, and American southerners often distinguish between singular *you* and plural *y'all*. Americans, Britons, and Australians learn to understand each other's accents merely by being exposed to them.

With its long history, rich heritage, and wide geographical distribution, Arabic naturally encompasses greater variation in its written and spoken forms than English. These differences present challenges to native speakers as well as to students of Arabic. You will need to learn some pronunciation variation, but these are easy to learn with listening practice. Sometimes you will need to learn two different words for the same concept. However, the more Arabic you learn, the more you will see that the overwhelming body of vocabulary and expressions are shared among most or all forms of Arabic.

Arabic consists of two registers, formal and spoken. Formal Arabic, also called Modern Standard or Classical Arabic, is learned in school rather than at home and is more a written than an oral register. It is highly respected and constitutes the "intellectual" register of Arabic. It is impossible to speak about topics of public interest, such as politics, economics, or even popular culture without using the vocabulary of formal Arabic. Hence, you will hear formal Arabic on news broadcasts and in other public contexts. However, educated speakers will often mix formal and spoken forms even in formal situations, because interacting with others in formal Arabic can seem impersonal.

Varieties of spoken Arabic, or colloquial dialects, are often designated by city, country, or region, such as Cairene, Moroccan, or Levantine (a term that refers to the Levant, and includes Syrian, Lebanese, Palestinian, and Jordanian dialects, which share most vocabulary and structure). However, some variations are social and might signal class or sectarian identity, whereas others distinguish rural and urban communities. The greatest variation in spoken Arabic is found in the most commonly used words in daily life, and what we call "accent"—the way certain sounds (especially vowels) are pronounced and words are stressed. For some examples of the similarities and differences in spoken Arabic, listen to four different regional varieties in Listening Exercise 2.

Listening Exercise 2. Dialect variation in Arabic (At home)

Listen to the sample phrases from four different dialects of Arabic. You will hear "good morning," "how are you?" "good," and "good-bye" each spoken in Tunisian, Egyptian, Lebanese, and Omani. Then you will hear each person say "I love Tunisia/ Egypt/Lebanon/Oman." Which phrases sound similar across dialects? Which sound completely different?

To be fluent in Arabic, you must have control of both the formal and spoken registers, including the mix that naturally occurs in academic and other intellectual discussions. As you learn more and more Arabic, you will see that the majority of words and structures are shared among varieties and registers, and you will learn to transfer knowledge from one variety to another.

In this textbook program we will introduce both formal and spoken forms of Arabic. The interactive media contain Egyptian dialogues filmed in Cairo and Levantine dialogues filmed in Damascus. In addition, the vocabulary and expressions that these dialogues contain are presented in Egyptian, Levantine, and formal Arabic. There are no dialogues in formal Arabic because this register is not used for social interaction in real life. The materials thus permit both learners and instructors to choose the variety they want to activate. Listening to two or even to all three forms will help you understand more Arabic, but with the guidance of your instructor, you should choose one variety as the one you will learn to use actively. In this way you will build both recognition and production skills. Both skills are important, and distinguishing between words you will recognize and those you will actively use will make the wealth of material more manageable.

A Transliteration System

It takes about twenty-five class hours plus at least fifty homework hours to master the Arabic alphabet and sound system introduced in this curriculum. We want you to spend a lot of this time learning and practicing basic greetings and expressions so that you can start speaking right away. In the beginning you will need a system of transliteration, or way of representing Arabic sounds and words in the Latin alphabet, so that you can start to study the vocabulary. We have devised a simplified system that we use for words that you cannot write in Arabic because you have not yet learned all the letters in them. We recommend that you learn and use this system unless you are a trained linguist and have another system you prefer. However, using transliteration should be a temporary, transitional stage. You should start writing words in Arabic script as soon as you learn all the letters. It will take longer to write words using Arabic script at first, but using it is the only way to develop proficiency in reading and writing, and with practice your writing speed will pick up.

The key to a good transliteration system is that each different sound should have its own unique symbol. Contrast this to English spelling, in which one letter represents many sounds, like *s* in *sun*, *prism*, and *treasure*, or one sound can be represented by different letters, like the sound *f*, also spelled *gh* in *laugh* and *ph* in *philosophy*. English vowel sounds and spellings are particularly fraught with ambiguities: the *u* in *but* sounds quite different from the *u* in *duty*, and *o* sounds quite different in *dot*, *one*, *OK*, and *office*. English uses the combination *th* to spell two different sounds, whereas these are distinct letters in Arabic. The following exercise will help you learn to distinguish these two sounds and learn to separate sound from English spelling.

Drill 1. Differentiating the *th* sounds (At home)

Distinguish between the sound *th* in the word *three* and *th* in the word *other*. These are two different sounds, and in Arabic they are written with different letters. Look at the list of words and repeat each one out loud several times to determine whether *th* sounds like *three* or *that*, and assign the word to the appropriate box.

they	thumb	teeth	there	throb	thus
although	think	through	brother	together	thought
weather	bother	theft	then	depth	rather

<u>three</u>	<u>that</u>
thumb thought teeth think throb theft think depth through	they weather there bother thus then although rather brother together

Most of the transliteration systems in use among specialists contain special symbols to indicate distinctly Arabic sounds (the Library of Congress system is one example of these). The technologies of texting and chatting mean that more and more Arabic speakers are communicating in Arabic with Latin script, and new transliteration patterns are emerging that include numerals. Can you see why the following correspondences have become popular?

3 ع   6 ط   7 ح

The transliteration system used in these materials is shown in the following charts. We developed this system to be simple, and the main difference between it and other systems is that it uses uppercase letters rather than dots and symbols to represent emphatic sounds, and we use doubled vowels *aa, ee, ii, oo,* and *uu* to represent long vowels. Listen to the pronunciation of letters on the alphabet videos again as you go through the consonant sounds in the first chart below.

Consonants:

Transliteration symbol and sound		Arabic letter	Transliteration symbol and sound		Arabic letter
z	as in *zip*	ز	b	as in *bet*	ب
s	as in *sip*	س	t	as in *tip*	ت
sh	as in *she*	ش	th	as in *three*	ث
S	emphatic S similar to *s* in *subtle*	ص	j	j or g, varies according to region	ج
D	emphatic D close to the *d* in *duh!*	ض	H	a raspy, breathy *h*	ح
T	emphatic T similar to *t* in *bottle*	ط	kh	like a German or Hebrew *ch*	خ
DH	emphatic DH close to *th* in *thy*	ظ	d	as in *dip*	د
c	a sound produced deep in the throat	ع	dh	th in *the* and *other*	ذ
gh	like French or Hebrew *r*	غ	r	like Spanish or Italian *r*	ر

Transliteration symbol and sound		Arabic letter
n	as in *neat*	ن
h	as in *aha!*	هـ
w	as in *wow!*	و
y	as in *yes*	ي
'	the sound you hear between vowels in *uh-oh!* (glottal stop)	ء

Transliteration symbol and sound		Arabic letter
f	as in *fun*	ف
q	like *k* but deeper in the throat	ق
k	as in *keep*	ك
l	like Spanish or Italian *l*	ل
m	as in *mat*	م

The next two charts give the vowel sounds. Formal Arabic has only three vowel sounds that are normally represented as *a*, *i*, and *u*, and each can be short or long. However, spoken Arabic has an expanded system that includes two additional vowel qualities, which we will indicate with *e* and *o*. In addition, Levantine pronunciation sometimes uses a *schwa* sound, which we will indicate with the *schwa* symbol, ə, which indicates a very short, unstressed vowel sound. Arabic distinguishes between short and long vowel sounds, and we will indicate length by repeating the vowel, as the chart shows. Pay particular attention to vowel sounds because they help you to distinguish emphatic consonants from their nonemphatic counterparts.

Vowels:

Transliteration symbol and sound	Short	Long	Arabic letter Short	Arabic letter Long
ranges from *e* in *bet* to *a* in *father*	a	aa	ـَ	ا
i as in *bit* (short) *ie* as in *piece* (long)	i	ii	ـِ	ي
oo as in *poodle*	u	uu	ـُ	و

Additional vowel sounds in spoken Arabic (not written):

French *é* as in *fiancé*	e	ee
o similar to *à la mode*	o	oo
e in *listen* (schwa)	ə	-

This transliteration system will be used to introduce words in new vocabulary lists while you are learning the letters. The only words that are transliterated are those that contain letters you have not yet learned. Remember that transliteration does not take the place of listening to the vocabulary on the interactive media. By listening and repeating new words several times, you will learn them well.

Drill 2. Reading in transliteration (In class)

The words in the following list are names of places you should be familiar with. With a partner, sound them out and identify as many as you can.

1. **amriika** America
2. **afghaanistaan** Afghanistan
3. **lubnaan** lebanon
4. **faransa** France
5. **as-saᶜuudiyya** Saudi Arabia
6. **al-yaabaan** Japan
7. **al-kuwayt**
8. **tuunis**
9. **ruusiyaa**
10. **as-suudaan**
11. **briiTaaniyaa**
12. **al-ᶜiraaq**
13. **al-hind** India
14. **ᶜumaan** Oman
15. **ifriiqiyaa**
16. **al-maksiik** Mexico
17. **al-yaman**
18. **iiTaaliyaa**
19. **abuu DHabii**
20. **isbaaniyaa** Spain
21. **al-urdunn** Jordan

🎧 Drill 3. Where is Arabic spoken? (At home)

The map shows countries where Arabic is the main language of education and where it is widely spoken in everyday life. You will see the names of the Arab countries and their capitals in English. Listen to the audio to hear the name and capital of each country in Arabic, and choose ten to write out using our transliteration system.

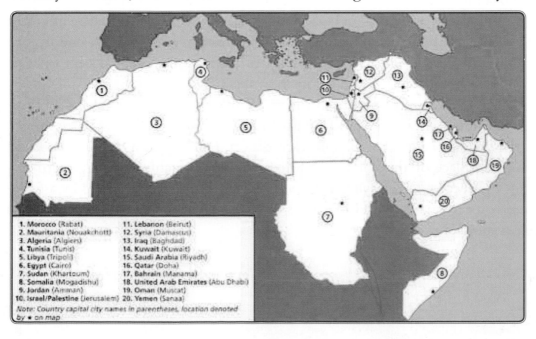

1. Morocco (Rabat)
2. Mauritania (Nouakchott)
3. Algeria (Algiers)
4. Tunisia (Tunis)
5. Libya (Tripoli)
6. Egypt (Cairo)
7. Sudan (Khartoum)
8. Somalia (Mogadishu)
9. Jordan (Amman)
10. Israel/Palestine (Jerusalem)
11. Lebanon (Beirut)
12. Syria (Damascus)
13. Iraq (Baghdad)
14. Kuwait (Kuwait)
15. Saudi Arabia (Riyadh)
16. Qatar (Doha)
17. Bahrain (Manama)
18. United Arab Emirates (Abu Dhabi)
19. Oman (Muscat)
20. Yemen (Sanaa)

Note: Country capital city names in parentheses, location denoted by ● on map

Vocabulary and Conversation: Greetings and Introductions

At least one section in each unit of *Alif Baa* is devoted to building vocabulary and speaking skills. Vocabulary is presented in the interactive media as well as in the book. You will refer to the vocabulary list in the book from time to time, but it is essential that you first learn it by using the interactive media so that you can hear and copy accurate pronunciation. You will remember vocabulary more readily if you repeat it out loud several times rather than read silently or listen passively. A good rule of thumb is to say each word out loud as many times as it takes to make it feel comfortable in your mouth and for you to be able to "hear" yourself say it.

Egyptian and Levantine Colloquial

The decision to include three varieties of Arabic in these materials rests on our conviction that competence in Arabic necessarily entails mastery of both spoken and formal registers. We have chosen Egyptian and Levantine because they are the most widely understood dialects across the Arab world. Levantine is a collection of dialects with many local flavors, but the pronunciation differences are small compared with the large amount of shared vocabulary and structure. The "flavor" of Levantine that you will hear in the dialogues is that of Damascus. Egyptian is represented by the dialect of Cairo, which is well-known from the films and music from the largest entertainment industry in the Arab world.

Each vocabulary chart contains three columns: formal, Levantine colloquial (or shaami), and Egyptian colloquial (or maSri). The shaami and maSri words are indicated in different colors throughout the materials. Our intention is for you to choose one spoken variety to master, but you might want to listen to the other dialect once to develop passive comprehension and recognition skills.

You will notice that most of the words you will learn are shared among all three varieties, sometimes with a slight shift in accent or a vowel. You will soon develop a sense of the characteristics that identify each dialect. For Egyptian, these include the hard *g* sound in place of the *j* of other dialects, and a distinctive accent pattern that emphasizes the second-to-last syllable. Levantine dialects are distinguished by a final *e* vowel sound on certain nouns and adjectives where other dialects have *a*, and their own distinctive intonation.

🎧 New Vocabulary (At home)

Listen to these greetings and repeat each one many times until you can say it easily. Choose one greeting and prepare to use it in class, and prepare to introduce yourself to others.

Meaning	maSri (Egyptian)	shaami (Levantine)	Formal /written
Greetings! (Islamic greeting)	السَّلامُ عَلَيكُم issalaamu ᶜalaykum	السَّلامُ عَلَيكُم assalaamu ᶜalaykum	السَّلامُ عَلَيكُم assalaamu ᶜalaykum
Hello! or Hi! (used more in Egypt than in the Levant)	أهلاً ahlan	أهلا ahla	أهلاً ahlan
Hello!	أهلاً وسَهلاً ahlan wa sahlan	أهلا وسَهلا ahla w sahla	أهلاً وسَهلاً ahlan wa sahlan
Hello! (used in the Levant)		مَرحَبا marHaba	مَرحَباً marHaban
I	أَنا ana	أَنا ana	أَنا ana
my name	اِسمي ismi	اِسمي ismi	اِسمي ismii
from	مِن min	مِن min	مِن min
the city of ...	مدينة midiinit	مدينة madiinit	مدينة madiinat
in	في fi	بِـ bi	في fii

Video Dialogues

In every unit there will be at least one video dialogue in both Egyptian and Levantine Arabic. We recommend that you choose one to learn actively, though you may choose to watch both varieties for the exposure and for comprehension practice. It is important to study the vocabulary from these dialogues before watching them, and to watch them at home before coming to class. The dialogues have three purposes: (a) to give you some speech models to imitate so you can start speaking; (b) to show you some aspects of polite interaction in Arab culture; and (c) to develop listening comprehension skills that you will use in class and in the real world, skills that help you understand what people are saying without knowing all the words they are using. You will find instructions for steps to take as you listen to these dialogues, and these steps are meant to help you reactivate and exploit the same listening strategies you used subconsciously to learn your native language. Each time you listen, you will get more out of the dialogue, especially if you set some specific goals and expectations for each "listen" ("listen," as usual, here is meant as a step; you will find it helpful to listen more than once at each stage, especially in the beginning). The final listen should take place after you have understood all you can, and it is the "activation" listen, in which you pay attention not to what is being said (because you presumably already know that), but rather to how it is being said, in pronunciation, vocabulary, and structure. In this activity, which should take place in class, you are preparing to use material from the dialogue in your own interactions with your classmates. Drill 4 below introduces the first dialogue. For this time only, listen to it in class with your instructor.

Drill 4. Scene 1: Ahlan wa sahlan (Formal and Colloquial) (In class)

In scene 1, people from across the Arab world introduce themselves. There are two versions, one formal Arabic and one spoken Arabic. Choose one to start with and watch it several times according to the following steps:

1. Before listening, ask yourself, "What do I expect to hear?"
2. First listen: Listen to see if your expectations are met. What do you hear?
3. Second listen: Which greetings do you recognize?
4. Third listen: What kinds of information do the speakers give? How do they express it, and what do you notice about the phrasing?
5. Fourth listen: Activate some of what you learned by introducing yourself to some of your classmates.
6. After you have understood and activated the variety you chose to begin with, listen to the other variety. What similarities and differences do you notice?

Culture: Saying Hello

Polite behavior requires you to say hello to everyone in a room or place you enter. The same principle also applies to a loosely defined "space" that someone regularly occupies, such as an outdoor work area or a guard's position outside a building. When you enter a space that is occupied, you must say hello. Whether or not you greet a guard or shopkeeper as you pass by depends primarily on your gender. In general, women do not say hello to men they do not know if they are not conducting business with them. Practice polite behavior by always saying hello to anyone in the room when you enter your Arabic class.

الوحدة الثانية
Unit Two

In this unit:

Consonants ب ت ث

Vowels ـَ ـُ ـِ ا و ي

Vocabulary and Conversation:
Meeting People

Culture: Shaking Hands

>> Letters and Sounds

١ aa (alif)

The name of the first letter of the Arabic alphabet is alif. Alif has two functions, the first of which will be introduced here, and the second will be discussed in unit 3. Here we are concerned with its function as a long vowel whose pronunciation ranges in sound from the *e* in *bet* to the *a* in *bat* to the *u* in *but*. Say these three words aloud and notice the difference in the quality of the vowels: the first is pronounced in the front of the mouth, the second slightly lower, and the last low in the mouth. The pronunciation of alif has a similar range; we refer to these differences in pronunciation as vowel quality. Two factors influence the vowel quality of alif: regional dialect and surrounding consonants.

In the eastern regions of the Arab world such as the Arabian Peninsula and Iraq, the sound of alif is generally deeper, similar to *father*, whereas farther west, especially in North Africa, it tends to be frontal and at times it approximates the sound of *e* in *bet*. You will notice this regional variation when you interact with Arabic speakers from different countries.

The other reason for variation in the quality of alif has to do with surrounding consonants. Arabic has several "emphatic" consonant sounds that are pronounced farther back in the mouth, and these consonants deepen the sound of a neighboring alif so that it resembles the *u* in *but*. Learning to discern and produce this difference in vowel quality will help you understand, speak, and write Arabic accurately. The following exercises will get you started, but remember to keep paying attention to vowel quality as you work through this book.

🎧 Listening Exercise 1. Frontal and deep alif (At home)

To hear the frontal and deep variants of alif, listen to the following pairs of words by clicking on them. The first word in each pair contains a frontal alif that contrasts with the deep alif in the second. Listen to and repeat these sounds aloud several times until you can hear the difference clearly and produce it.

١. تاب / طاب   ٢. ساح / صاح

٣. داني / ضاني   ٤. ذال / ظالم

The first word of each pair in Listening Exercise 1 begins with a consonant sound familiar to speakers of English, and the second word begins with a deeper sound that resembles the first but is pronounced with the tongue lower and farther back in the mouth. These deeper sounds are often called emphatic consonants, and they affect the pronunciation of surrounding vowel sounds. Listening for the difference between frontal and deep alif is the best way to distinguish between emphatic and nonemphatic consonants. We will discuss this point in more depth in unit 5, when you begin to learn the emphatic letters.

Drill 1. Hearing frontal and deep alif (At home)

Each word you will hear contains an alif. Say the word aloud as you listen to it and decide whether the alif is frontal or deep. Select F if the alif is frontal and D if it is deep.

1. D F   2. D F   3. D F   4. D F

5. D F   6. D F   7. D F   8. D F

9. D F   10. D F   11. D F   12. D F

In addition to vowel quality, Arabic also distinguishes vowel length, and this too can affect the meaning of a word. In Listening Exercise 1, you can hear that the alif is a long vowel. In the very last word, DHaalim, you can hear the contrast in vowel length between the long alif in the first syllable and the short vowel *i* in the second. Notice that the stress or word accent in DHaalim is on the first syllable, the one with alif. Long vowels attract word stress in Arabic. We will practice hearing and pronouncing this distinction later in this unit.

Writing

The letters above are, from right to left, the independent, initial, medial, and final shapes of the letter alif. In this section you will learn to write the various shapes of the letter alif. Watch calligrapher and professor of Arabic Sayyid El-Shinnawi write the shapes of alif as you read and write this section, and learn to draw the letters using the same hand motions he does.

Alone or at the beginning of a word, the alif is written as a single stroke, drawn from top to bottom, as the arrow in the example shows. Practice on the blank lines below, copying the example on the first line, pronouncing alif as you write it as many times as you can in the space provided:

When the alif follows another letter, it is written from the bottom up. The previous letter will end in a connecting segment drawn on the line. Start with that segment, then draw the alif from the bottom up as shown:

In both cases the alif does not connect to what follows it. Always pick your pen up from the page after writing alif.

Now practice reading alif by circling all of the alifs you can find in the following sentence (taken from *1001 Nights*):

كان يا ما كان في قديم الزمان، كان تاجر كثير المال والاعمال ...

baa

The second letter of the Arabic alphabet is pronounced like *b* in English. This consonant lends a frontal quality to vowels.

🎧 Listening Exercise 2. Pronouncing ب (At home)

Listen to and repeat the words containing ب , focusing on the frontal quality of the vowels.

1. باء   2. باب   3. لبنان   4. ليبيا   5. بيت   6. حب

🎧 Writing

بـ   ـبـ   ـب   ب   ب

The independent, initial, medial, and final shapes of the letter baa all share an initial "tooth" and a single dot below the line. Watch Professor El-Shinnawi write the shapes of this letter as you read and write this section, and imitate his hand movements. Unlike alif, this is a connecting letter, which means that it connects to any letter following it in the same word. The main parts of the letter, the initial tooth and the dot beneath the body, remain constant in all four shapes. Compare the independent and final shapes, and note that both end in a second tooth. Think of this tooth as the "tail" of the letter that is used when it occurs at the end of a word. It is not written in initial and medial positions because the letter ب always connects to the following letter in those cases.

When written alone, this letter takes the independent shape shown above. Following the steps shown in the example on the first line below, trace the letter with your pencil a few times, and then write it. First, write the body: from right to left, begin with a small hook, then continue straight along the line and end with another hook for the tail. After you have finished the body, place the dot below the letter as shown (you can associate the sound *b* with the dot *below* the letter). Copy and practice:

When followed by another letter, it connects to that letter by deleting the final hook: ـب. When writing this and other connecting dotted letters, you should place the dot more or less in vertical alignment with the initial tooth of the letter. The exact length of the body and placement of the dot may vary somewhat according to the style of the hand-writing or print font; study the various styles you see and imitate the one that suits you.

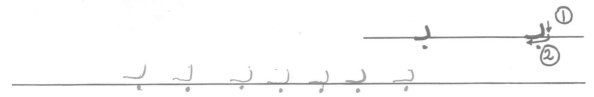

Now write the first two letters of the alphabet joined together: ـبا . Do not pick up the pen to cross the ب until you have finished writing the alif joined to it. Copy the example and pronounce it aloud:

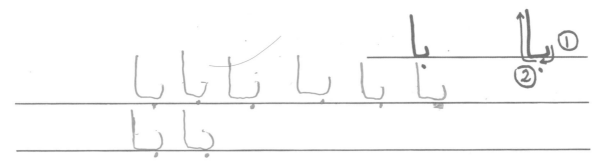

When ـبـ occurs in medial position, connecting segments link it to previous and following ones as shown. (This will become clearer when you learn a few more letters.) Copy the example:

Final ــب resembles the independent form with the final hook. This form may be illustrated by writing two ب's together: بب. Copy the example:

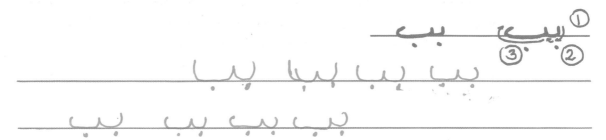

Now you can write your first word in Arabic: باب *door*. Practice writing this word by copying the example shown below, pronouncing it out loud as you write. Remember: Do not stop to dot the letters until you have finished the skeletal structure of the entire word.

As you work through this book, remember to pronounce the words and expressions you write out loud as you write them, preferably more than once. Develop the habit of writing and saying words out loud simultaneously rather than writing silently. This practice helps to reinforce the connection between sound and shape, to build reading skills, and to memorize vocabulary faster.

taa

The third letter of the alphabet is pronounced like a clear, frontal English *t*. How many different ways do you pronounce *t*? Read the following list aloud the way you would normally pronounce the words when speaking: *bottle, teeth, automatic*. Of these words, most American speakers pronounce the *t* in *teeth* forward in the mouth, against the back of the teeth. This is the correct position of the tongue (and not the flap of the tongue you use to produce *bottle* and *automatic*) for the pronunciation of this Arabic sound. Arabic ت must be pronounced with the tip of your tongue against your teeth but without aspiration.[1] Since ت is a frontal letter, the vowel sounds surrounding it are frontal too; in particular, the alif sounds like *e* as in *bet* (and not like *u* in *but*).

🎧 Listening Exercise 3. Pronouncing ت (At home)

Listen to the sound of the letter ت and repeat. Pay attention to the position of your tongue as you do so and notice the frontal quality of the vowels.

1. تاء   2. بات   توت .3   4. وتد   بنت .5   6. شتاء

🎧 Writing

M   I   Standard

ت

Watch Professor El-Shinnawi and imitate his movements as you read and write this section. This letter has the same shapes as the ب in all positions, and it is also a connector. Instead of one dot underneath, however, it is written with two dots above its body ت (you can associate the sound *t* with *two dots on top*). In printed text the two dots are separated, as you see. In handwriting, however, they are often run together into a short horizontal bar (this depends in part on individual practice. Try to write two dots quickly and you will see how this handwriting form developed.) Practice writing the independent ت by copying the example:

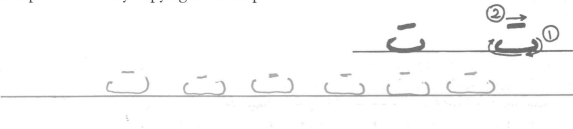

---

[1]Aspiration refers to the breathy sound often heard with *t*, *p*, and *k*. Light a match, hold it in front of your mouth, and say, "Peter, Tom, and Kirk went to town." The flame will flicker each time you pronounce one of these letters. Arabic sounds do not have aspiration, so practice saying *t* and *k* with a lit match in front of your mouth until you can pronounce them without making the flame flicker.

Practice writing ت in initial and medial positions by copying the word تتب (*tatub*) as shown:

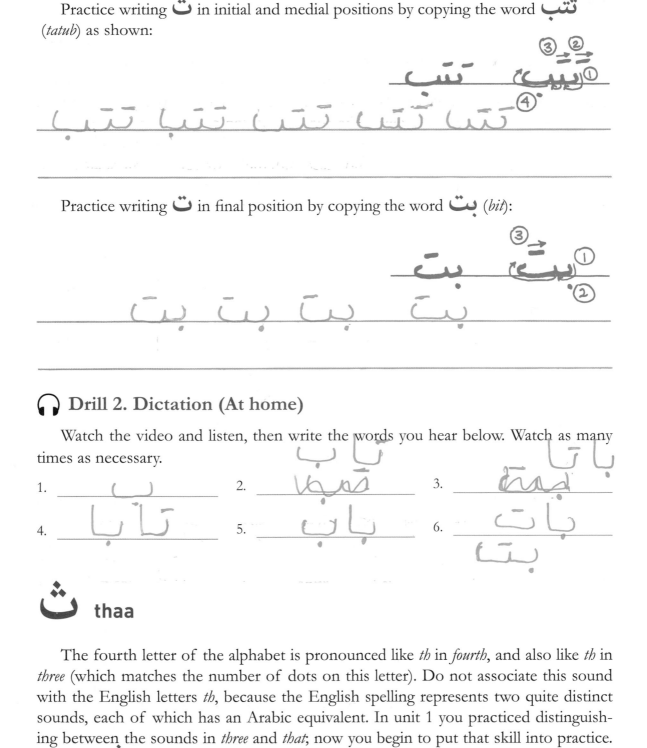

Practice writing ت in final position by copying the word بت (*bit*):

🎧 Drill 2. Dictation (At home)

Watch the video and listen, then write the words you hear below. Watch as many times as necessary.

1. _____
2. _____
3. _____
4. _____
5. _____
6. _____

ث thaa

The fourth letter of the alphabet is pronounced like *th* in *fourth*, and also like *th* in *three* (which matches the number of dots on this letter). Do not associate this sound with the English letters *th*, because the English spelling represents two quite distinct sounds, each of which has an Arabic equivalent. In unit 1 you practiced distinguishing between the sounds in *three* and *that*; now you begin to put that skill into practice. The letter ث represents the sound in *three*, and not the sound in *that*. Remember this by reminding yourself that this letter has three dots, and say *three* out loud before pronouncing or reading ث.

🎧 Listening Exercise 4. Listening to ث (At home)

Listen to the sound of the letter ث in the following words and repeat.

5. بث   4. اثاث   3. تـثبت   2. ثابت   1. ثاء

🎧 Listening Exercise 5. Contrasting *th* and *dh* (At home)

Listen to the difference between the sound ث and the sound ذ *(dh)* in the following words. Listen to each pair several times until you can hear the difference clearly. Note also the frontal quality of both sounds.

3. آثار/آذار   2. بثور/بذور   1. ثاب/ذاب

5. جث/جذ   4. تثوب/تذوب

🎧 Writing

ﺚ   ﺛ   ﺚ   ث

This letter is a connector and is written just like ب and ت in all positions, except that it has three dots above. Watch Professor El-Shinnawi write ث and imitate his writing. Notice that he connects the three dots as a caret. In print the three dots appear as you see above but in handwriting the three dots are usually connected and written as a caret-shaped mark (which can be slightly rounded) as shown in the example below. Practice writing and saying independent ث :

Copy and practice initial ث in the male name ثابت *(thaabit)*:

Practice writing medial ـثـ in the word تثبت (*tathbut*):

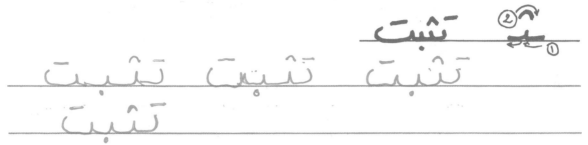

Write final ـث by copying the word تبث (*tabuth*):

🎧 **Drill 3. Word recognition (At home)**

Listen to the audio to hear a word, then decide which of the two words in each pair that you heard and select that word.

3. تاب / ثاب   2. بتات / ثبات   1. بات / باب

6. تبث / ثبت   5. ثابت / باثث   4. بث / تب

برافو! Bravo! You have learned the first four letters of the Arabic alphabet. The next letters in sequence will be presented in unit 3. Now we will skip ahead to the other two long vowels and the symbols for the corresponding short vowels

و uu

This letter represents the second of the three long vowels in Arabic. It is pronounced like the exclamation of delight: ooooo! Practice saying this sound and stretch it out, just like you would say the exclamation. Don't be afraid to exaggerate vowel length—it will help you get used to thinking about vowel length. **Remember that the pronunciation of و , like that of alif, should be twice as long as normal English vowels.**

🎧 Listening Exercise 6. Listening to and pronouncing و (At home)

Listen to and repeat the words containing و. Give its full length in pronunciation.

١. تـوت ٢. تـابـوت ٣. ثـبـوت ٤. تـونـس ٥. تحبـو

🎧 Writing

و ـو و ـو

Like alif, this letter does not connect to any following letter, and therefore its shapes do not vary much. To write independent or initial و, start on the line, loop clockwise to the left and up, then swing down into the tail, which should dip well below the line. Watch Professor El-Shinnawi and copy the example:

When writing و connected to a previous letter, the joining segment leads into the beginning point of the loop. Copy the example:

Now practice writing and pronouncing the word تـوت (*mulberries*):

 Drill 4. Dictation (At home)

Watch the video and listen, then write the words you hear below. Watch as many times as necessary.

1. ـَـنـب _____   2. تـوت _____

3. ثـوـنـب _____   4. ثـبـت _____

ي ii

This letter represents the last of the three long vowels, the sound of *ee* in *beep*. Remember that this is a long vowel; pronounce this sound for twice as long as you would pronounce *ee* in words like *beep*, *street*. Practice by imitating the sound of a honking car horn: beeeeep! Exaggerate it to focus on hearing and pronouncing vowel length.

 **Listening Exercise 7. Hearing and pronouncing ي** (At home)

Listen to and repeat the words containing ي, giving it full length in pronunciation.

4. تثبتـي   3. ليبـي   2. تثبيت   1. توبـي

 **Writing**

ي   يـ   ـيـ   ـي   ي

As you can see above, the independent and final forms of ي differ slightly from the initial and medial forms. Like ب، ت، and ث, which it resembles in its initial and

medial shapes, this letter is a connecting one. All shapes of ي retain the two dots below, but in handwriting, the two dots underneath are usually drawn as a short horizontal bar, just like the dots on top of ت.

To write independent ي , start above the line and curve slightly upwards and
around in an s-like shape. Continue below the line into a wide, flat curve as shown, and
make sure to bring the tail all the way back up over the line:

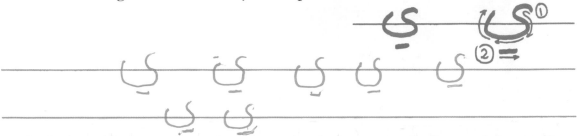

In final position start from the connecting segment on the line, and then make a
small hook into the body. In this position the letter is almost entirely below the line and
has only a small curved hook before dipping into the wide, flat curve. Practice copying
and pronouncing ـي and bring the tail all the way back up above the line:

When ي occurs at the beginning or in the middle of a word, it takes the same
shape as تـ , except that its two dots are below the body of the letter. Copy the example of initial يـ :

Now practice writing medial ـيـ in the word تثبيت *(tathbiit)*:

🎧 **Drill 5. Dictation (At home)**

Watch and listen to the video, then write below the words you hear.

1. _____ ثوبي _____ 2. _____ اسمي بيتي بيتي _____

3. _____ بيت _____ 4. _____ بنتي _____

>> # Short Vowels

‗ a (fatHa)   ُ u (Damma)   ‗ i (kasra)

Each of the long vowels ا, و, and ي has a short vowel that corresponds to it. These short vowels are shown above, where you can easily see and hear the correspondence: *aa* (alif) is the long vowel corresponding to *a* (fatHa), *uu* to *u* (Damma), and *ii* to *i* (kasra). The length of these short vowels corresponds to the length of most English vowels, and the length of the long vowels should be at least twice that of a short vowel. English has no long vowels so Arabic long vowels should sound and feel extra long to you. Do not worry about pronouncing a long vowel "too long"—stretch it out so that you can hear the difference. It is important to learn to distinguish between the two lengths in listening and in speaking because vowel length often makes a difference in meaning, or, if mispronounced, renders the word unintelligible.

Short vowels are indicated in Arabic script by symbols written above or below the consonant skeleton and dots. **Remember:** syllables in Arabic always begin with a consonant; by convention, short vowels are written above or below the consonant they follow. Writing vowels is the third and final step in writing a word, after both the consonant skeleton and the dots have been completed. Of course, as you learned in unit 1, short vowels are usually not written at all; you have been writing words without them so far. Remember that vowel length affects word stress. Syllables with long vowels are almost always accented (emphasized in pronunciation).[2]

The following exercises will help you learn to hear and produce the distinction between long and short vowels; work through them carefully and repeat until you are comfortable hearing this distinction.

🎧 Listening Exercise 8. Hearing vowel length (At home)

Listen to and pronounce the differences in vowel length in the pairs of words you hear. The first word in each pair contains a long vowel and the second word contains a short vowel.

3. شاب / شَب   2. توب / تُب   1. ساد / سَد

5. تقول / تقُل   4. بير / بِر

---

[2] For those with some linguistic training, note that in general, Arabic word stress falls on "heavy" syllables: syllables with a long vowel or consonant-vowel-consonant (as opposed to just consonant-short vowel). Word accent or stress will fall on the heavy syllable closest to the end of the word. If there is no heavy syllable, stress varies according to regional dialect. Egyptian word stress patterns are quite distinctive and usually fall on the penultimate syllable.

6/6

🎧 Drill 6. Distinguishing between long and short vowels (At home)

Listen to each pair of words and repeat several times until you can hear the difference between the long and short vowels. Select the letter that corresponds to the word that contains a long vowel.

1.   a   b   2.   a   b   3.   a   b
4.   a   b   5.   a   b   6.   a   b

🎧 Drill 7. Identifying long and short vowels (At home) 12/12

Listen to the audio to hear a selection of words. For each question, select L if you hear one of the long vowels ا , و , or ي, or S if the word has only short vowels (fatHa, Damma, or kasra).

1.   L   S   2.   L   S   3.   L   S   4.   L   S
5.   L   S   6.   L   S   7.   L   S   8.   L   S
9.   L   S   10.   L   S   11.   L   S   12.   L   S

´ a (fatHa)

The short vowel that corresponds to alif is called fatHa. Like its long counterpart alif, fatHa ranges in quality from frontal to deep, depending on the quality of the consonants surrounding it. In its most frontal position, fatHa sounds like English *e* as in *bet*. Deep fatHa sounds like English *u* in *but*. Consonants ب , ت , and ث are frontal ones, so they give fatHa a frontal quality, like *e* in *bet*. The name fatHa means "opening", and refers to the shape of the mouth in pronouncing it: open. Try it and see!

🎧 Listening Exercise 9. Contrasting alif and fatHa (At home)

Listen to and repeat the words containing alif and fatHa. Pay special attention to the difference in vowel length.

1. ثابَت   ثَبـات   2. تابَ   تاب   3. باتَت   4. تابَت   5. ثَبـات

🎧 Writing

´
—

Arabic words consist of syllables that always begin with consonants, followed by either a short or long vowel. Short vowels are written on top of the letter that precedes them, the first letter of the syllable. FatHa is written as a short, slanted line segment above its consonant, as in the word ثَبَتَ . Watch Professor El-Shinnawi write fatHa and copy the example:

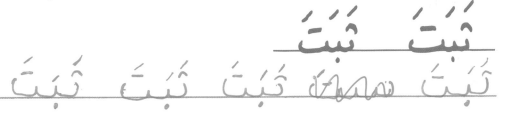

🎧 Drill 8. FatHa dictation (At home)

Listen to the words and write fatHa where you hear it.

1. تَثْبِيت 2. بَتات 3. باتَت

4. ثَبات 5. ثَبَت 6. ثابت

و
— u (Damma)

The short vowel that corresponds to و is called Damma and is pronounced like *oo* as in *booth* when it follows frontal consonants. When it is affected by deep consonants it is a little bit deeper, somewhat like *oo* in *wool*. Do not confuse this vowel with English *o* and *u*, which represent many different sounds, some of them closer to deep fatHa than to Damma. **Remember:** English *u* in words like *but* and *gum* actually represents the sound of a deep fatHa, not a Damma. The name Damma refers to the correct shape of the mouth in pronunciation: rounding. If you keep your mouth rounded, you will pronounce Damma correctly.

🎧 **Listening Exercise 10. Hearing and pronouncing Damma**

Listen to and repeat the words containing Damma, rounding your mouth as you do so. Listen for two words that contain both Damma and waaw and practice the difference in vowel length.

1. تُب	2. بُث	3. ثُبـوت
4. حُبوب	5. صُب	6. تَثبُت

🎧 **Writing**

و
▬

Damma is written like a miniature و on top of the letter that precedes it, as in the word تُب. Imitate the motions that Professor El-Shinnawi uses to draw Damma and practice writing ُ as shown:

▬ **i (kasra)**

The short vowel that corresponds to ي is called kasra, and its pronunciation ranges from frontal *ee* as in *keep* to deep *i* as in *bit*. As with fatHa and Damma, the exact pronunciation of kasra depends on surrounding consonants. Frontal consonants like ت and ث give kasra a frontal quality. The name kasra, "break", refers to the fact that your mouth is slightly open in pronouncing it (as opposed to the broad fatHa opening). Pronounce kasra and note that your mouth is slightly open, and not wide open.

🎧 Listening Exercise 11. Pronouncing kasra (At home)

Listen to and repeat the words that contain kasra.

3. بِت   2. تُثْبِتِي   1. ثِب

6. كِتَابِي   5. تُحِب   4. طِب

🎧 Writing

ِ

The kasra is written as a short, slanted line segment under the letter it follows, as in ثِب . Copy the example:

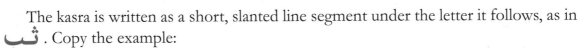

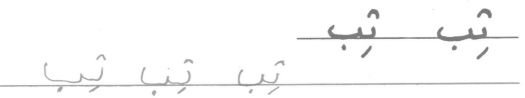

Drill 9. Letter recognition (In class)

To practice recognizing all the letters you have learned, go back to one of the vocalized texts in unit 1 (the Qur'an, the Bible, or the schoolbook) and, with a partner, identify as many letters as you can. Name the short vowels you see too.

🎧 Drill 10. Short vowel dictation (At home)

Listen and write all of the short vowels in the words you hear. Listen as many times as necessary.

3. تَبِيت   2. تُبِت   1. ثبِتِ

6. ثبوت   5. تِثبِت   4. تِتوب

🎧 Drill 11. Dictation (At home)

Watch and listen to the video and write below the words you hear including all vowels. Listen as many times as necessary.

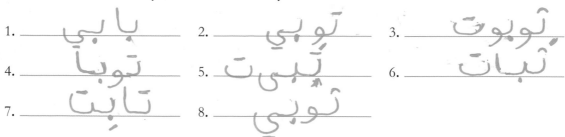

1. ــــــــــــ بابي

2. ــــــــــــ توبي

3. ــــــــــــ توبوت

4. ــــــــــــ توبا

5. ــــــــــــ تيبيت

6. ــــــــــــ تبات

7. ــــــــــــ تابت

8. ــــــــــــ توبي

🎧 Drill 12. Reading aloud (At-home preparation; in-class activation)

Read aloud each of the following words. Then listen to the audio to check your pronunciation.

1. بَث

2. بابي

3. تُثبِت

4. ثُب

5. ثَبات

6. تَبات

7. تابا

8. ثابِت

9. توبي

10. تِيتو

11. ثابَت

12. تَثبيت

Drill 13. Letter connection (At home)

Connect the letters to form words as shown in the example and pronounce them out loud as you write.

Example: تاب = ت + ا + ب

1. ب + ا + ت + ا = ــــــــــــ بَاتَا

2. ث + ب + ا + ت + ي = ــــــــــــ ثَباتي

3. ب + ا + ب + ا = ــــــــــــ بابا

4. ث + تَ + بَ + تَ = ــــــــــــ ثَبَتَ

5. ب + ا + ب + ي = ــــــــــــ بابي

6. ت + و + ب + ي = _____ توبي_____

7. تُ + ب + تَ = _____ تُبتَ_____

8. ت + و + ب + ا = _____ توبا_____

9. تُ + ث + بِ + ت + ي = _____ تُثبتي_____

10. تَ + ي + ب + ت = _____ تَيبت_____

11. ب + ي + ت + ي = _____ بيتي_____

>> Vocabulary and Conversation: Meeting People

 New Vocabulary (At home)

Listen to and learn these expressions that are used when meeting someone new. Select the dialect you are learning, Egyptian maSri or Levantine/Syrian shaami (the Arabic word shaami can mean Syrian, Damascene, or Levantine). Listen to and repeat each word many times until you can "hear" and pronounce each word easily. To use this vocabulary you need to know that Arabic omits the present tense verb *is/are*, so the question "What is your name?" will consist of *what* and *your name*, for example: **shuu ismak?** (Levantine), and **ismak ee?** (Egyptian, note that the word *"what?"* occurs at the end of the question in this dialect).

You will notice that this list includes two sets of words for "you", one identified as "polite": **HaDritak / HaDritik** or **HaDərtak / HaDərtik**. This polite form (which literally means "your presence") is used in situations where you want to show respect to the person you are talking to, especially in Egypt. You will hear this expression used in the dialogues; practice using it in class.

Meaning	maSri	shaami	Formal /written
door	باب	باب	باب
name	اِسم ism	اِسم ism	اِسم ism
what?	إيه؟ ee?	شو؟ shuu?	ما؟ maa?
(reply to) ahlan wa sahlan (to a male)	أهلاً بيك ahlan biik	أهلاً فيك ahlan fiik	أهلاً بكَ ahlan bika
(reply to) ahlan wa sahlan (to a female)	أهلاً بيكِ ahlan biiki	أهلاً فيكِ ahlan fiiki	أهلاً بكِ ahlan biki
(reply to) assalaamu ᶜalaykum	وعليكم السلام wa ᶜalaykumu s-salaam	وعليكم السلام wa ᶜalaykumu s-salaam	وعليكم السلام wa ᶜalaykumu s-salaam

Meaning	maSri		shaami		Formal /written	
you (polite form, to a male)	HaDritak	حَضِرتَك	HaDərtak	حَضِرتَك	HaDratuka	حَضِرتُكَ
you (polite form, to a female)	HaDritik	حَضِرتِك	HaDərtik	حَضِرتِك	HaDratuki	حَضِرتُكِ
Nice to meet you!	itsharrafna	اِتشَرَّفنا	tsharrafna	تشَرَّفنا	tasharrafnaa	تَشَرَّفنا
you (masculine)	inta	إنتَ	inte	إنتِ	anta	أنتَ
you (feminine)	inti	إنتِ	inti	إنتِ	anti	أنتِ
my (possessive suffix) my name	–i ismi	– ي اِسمي	–i ismi	– ي اِسمي	–i ismii	– ي اِسمي
your (suffix, masculine) your name	–ak ismak	– َك اِسمَك	–ak ismak	– َك اِسمَك	–ka or –k ismuka	– كَ اِسمُكَ
your (suffix, feminine) your name	–ik ismik	– ِك اِسمِك	–ik ismik	– ِك اِسمِك	–ki ismuki	– كِ اِسمُكِ
where?	feen?	فين؟	ween?	وين؟	ayna?	أَيْنَ؟
from where?	mineen?	منين؟	min ween?	من وين؟	min ayna?	مِن أَيْنَ؟
yes	aywa	أَيوَه	ee	إيه	naᶜam	نَعَم
no	la'	لا	la', laa	لا	laa	لا

Drill 14. Meet someone new (At-home preparation; in-class activation)

At home, actively study the new vocabulary by rehearsing the greetings and questions that you will ask your classmates. You can write them out but you will not be able to read from the paper in class, so remember to practice out loud. In class, go around the room and greet all of your classmates one by one, and if you do not know their names, find out!

Drill 15. Listen and interact (At home)

On the audio you will hear someone initiate a conversation with you. Respond out loud to the person's questions using as much Arabic as you can. More than one response is possible, so you can do this exercise as many times as you want to practice interacting.

Drill 16. Cities in Egypt and Syria (At-home preparation; in-class activation)

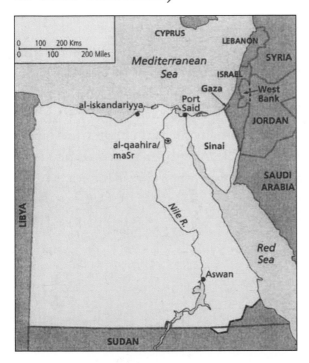
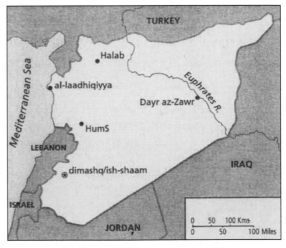

The maps above show the major cities in Egypt and Syria. You will hear the Arabic names of some of these cities in the dialogues. Use the internet to find out more about one or two of them and report to your classmates.

🎧 **Drill 17. Scene 2:** *HaDritak min maSr? / inti min ween?*
   (At-home preparation; in-class activation)

Watch scene 2 according to these steps:

1. First listen: What are the two people doing?
    Do they know each other? How do you know?
2. Second listen: What words and expressions do you hear this time?
3. Before listening a third time, prepare your questions.
    What parts of the exchange do you want to understand more of?
    What do you think is happening in that section?
    Based on this hypothesis, what words and expressions do you expect to hear?
    Write what you think was said.
4. In class, discuss the scene and go over any questions, then listen once more for activation, and act out the scene with your classmates.

Culture: Shaking hands

In social as well as in professional situations, it is polite to shake hands upon meeting or greeting another person of the same gender. The appropriateness of shaking hands with the opposite gender varies widely according to religious beliefs and personal practice. If you are a male meeting a female, it is better to wait for her to extend her hand first, indicating that she wants to shake yours. In many regions children are taught to greet older, respected guests by shaking hands and leaning over to kiss or be kissed on both cheeks to welcome them into the home with warmth and respect.

الوحدة الثالثة
Unit Three

In this unit:

Letters خ ح ج

و and ي as consonants

sukuun ـْ

Vocabulary and Conversation:
Greeting people

Culture:
Expressions *SabaaH il-khayr!* and *al-Hamdu li-llaah!*

Letters and Sounds

The three new consonants you will learn in this unit represent the next three letters in the alphabet after ث . Just as ب , ت , and ث share the same skeletal shape and are distinguished by the number and position of the dots, so these three letters have the same basic shapes and are distinguished by their dots. Two of these three consonant sounds have no English equivalent. You can learn to pronounce them properly by practicing every day to develop the muscles you need to pronounce these sounds.

ج jiim / giim

The letter jiim has three pronunciations that vary according to region across the Arab world. In Iraq, the Gulf, and in many rural and Bedouin dialects, it is pronounced like *j* in *jack*. In most of the Levant region and North Africa, it is pronounced like the French *j* in *bonjour* (a sound often represented in English by *s*, as in *pleasure* or *decision*). In Cairo, it is pronounced like the hard *g* in *game*.

Listening Exercise 1. Variation of ج (At home)

Listen to the words as they are pronounced in the three dialect variations of ج.

1. تـاج   2. جُب   3. تُجِيب   4. دَجاج

Learn to recognize all three pronunciations of ج, and choose one to use when speaking. It is a good idea to choose at least one voice model to imitate for speaking in general, whether a teacher, friend or acquaintance, or some of the characters in the colloquial scenes. Choose the pronunciation of ج that your voice model uses.

Writing

These letters show the shapes of ج and its sister letters in print. Notice that the independent and final shapes (first and last above) have a big "tail" that curves well below the line. In all positions the body of the letter retains its basic form that you see in the initial shape. The medial form shows what the ـجـ looks like when it is connected on both sides. However, in handwriting, this letter and its sisters are connected in a different way than in print. Watch Professor El-Shinnawi write the shapes of ج and similar letters as you learn to write these letters and imitate the handwritten forms, not the print ones.

As the initial and medial shapes of this letter suggest, ح is a connector. To write ح alone, start at a point well above the line, make a small hook, then draw a line straight across, then change direction and swing down below the line into the tail. Follow the arrows and imitate the shape that you see:

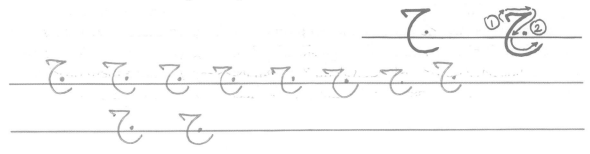

To write ج in initial position, begin with the hook as you did above, then slant down toward the line into a point just above the line, and then, instead of curving down into the tail, continue into the connecting segment as shown:

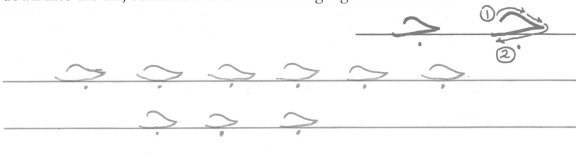

Practice writing the word جاب *(he brought)*:

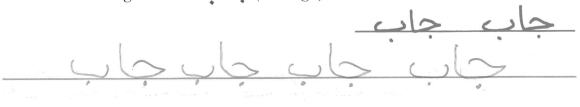

When this letter is connected on both sides, it takes the shape ـجـ in printed text, as in تُجِيب *(she answers)*. **However, it is not written this way by hand.** Watch Professor El-Shinnawi write this shape and look at the example below. To write this letter in second position, after an initial, you must plan ahead because the connecting segment lies well above the line, at the highest point of this letter. This means that you need to end the previous letter above the line. As you can see, the combination تج is written by starting and drawing the تـ completely above the line and then dropping down into the ـجـ. You will notice that Professor El-Shinnawi draws the "tooth" of the initial ت upside down; this is a sophisticated calligraphic style used by some people when they write. Copy the word تُجِيب as it is written here:

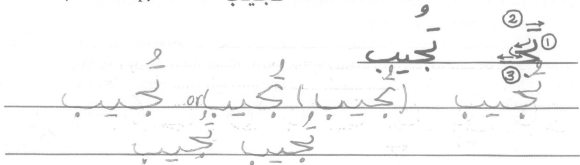

To reach the starting point of a medial or final ج, a connecting segment is drawn from the line up and then over as the example shows. In word-final position, ج takes the same tail it has in the independent position. Watch Professor El-Shinnawi and copy the word بِيج *(beige)*:

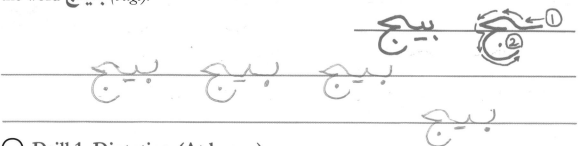

🎧 Drill 1. Dictation (At home)

Using the video, write below the words you hear, including all vowels. Watch and listen as many times as necessary.

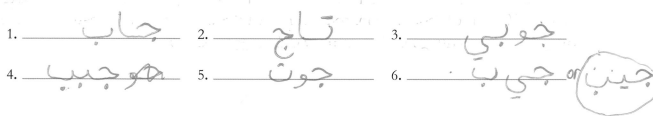

1. _____ جَاب _____ 2. _____ تَاج _____ 3. _____ جُوبِي

4. _____ هُجِيب _____ 5. _____ جُوت _____ 6. _____ جِيب or جِيب

ح Haa

The letter Haa represents a sound that is pronounced deep in the throat. It has no equivalent in English. First, take a few minutes to become better acquainted with some of the throat muscles that you use often but not to speak English. The following exercise is designed to make you aware of what these muscles can already do so that you can use them to speak Arabic. Practice this exercise as often as you can over the next two weeks or so until you can do it easily and your pronunciation of ح has developed.

Pronouncing ح : With your mouth open, make a raspy, breathy sound like an exaggerated *h*, or like you are breathing on glass in order to make it fog up. Put your hand on your throat as you do this, and notice that your throat muscles are not moving at all.

To pronounce ح , you need to activate those muscles by tightening them on the inside so that you are constricting the air passage and blocking off air from the inside. You should be able to feel the Adam's apple move. Make more raspy *h* sounds. Constrict the muscles so that air can just barely squeeze through your throat. When you do this successfully, it will produce ح . Keep practicing contracting and relaxing the muscles using your hand to guide you. Most important, repeat this exercise as often as you can. Pronouncing ح takes practice and concentration at first. The more you practice now, the sooner you will be able to say it easily. It is important to pronounce this sound correctly to distinguish it from the English *h*, which is a different letter in Arabic, because this difference affects meaning.

🎧 **Listening Exercise 2. Pronouncing ح (At home)**

Listen to the sound of ح in various positions and repeat until your pronunciation matches that of the speaker.

1. حَبيب   بَحث .2   تَبوح .3   صَباح .4

🎧 **Writing**

ـح   ـحـ   حـ   ح

Like ج , the letter ح is a connector. It is written exactly like ج , except that it has no dot. Watch Professor El-Shinnawi and imitate the way he writes the various shapes of ح . Practice writing initial ح in the word حبيب *(darling)*:

Now practice writing and pronouncing medial ـحـ in تَحْت *(below)* **as it is written by hand** (not in print). Remember to plan ahead and write the preceding letter above the line so that you can connect ـحـ from above. Copy the example:

Sometimes two of these letters occur together in juxtaposition. Here, too, you must give yourself room to connect into the second letter by writing the first one well above the line. Do not break the skeletal structure of the word by lifting your pen. Copy the example and practice writing حِجاب *(veil, hijab)*:

تُبيح

tubeeh

Final ـح is written with the tail. Copy the word تُبيح as it is written, starting above the line to give yourself room to connect down into the ح :

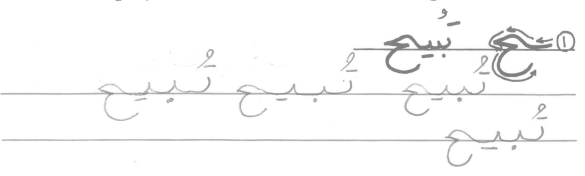

🎧 **Drill 2. Dictation** (At home)

Using the video, write below the words you hear, including all vowels. Watch and listen as many times as necessary.

بَحَثَ

1. _____ حوث _____   2. _____ لعصا _____   3. _____ حَبِيب _____

4. _____ تَحتَ _____   5. _____ يوحي _____   6. _____ باجات باحَت _____

رُوحي

خ **khaa**

The sound of the letter khaa is found in many European languages: the Russian *x*, the Scottish pronunciation of *loch*, and German *ch* as in *Bach*. To pronounce خ, say *k* and pay attention to where the back of your tongue hits the back of the roof of your mouth and cuts off the air flow (the blocking and release is what makes the *k* sound). Instead of closing off the air flow with the back of your tongue completely, block it part way and you will be able to produce this sound.

Listening Exercise 3. Pronouncing خ (At home)

Listen to and repeat these words containing خ.

5. تَختي   4. بَخت   3. باخ   2. بَخيل   1. خاب

🎧 **Writing**

خ   ـخ   ـخـ   خ   خ

Like its sisters, خ is a connector and its shapes are written exactly as the ones you learned for ج and ح, except that it takes one dot above. Practice writing initial خ in the word خاب, saying it as you write:

② ① خاب

خ خ خاب خاب خاب خاب

Practice writing and pronouncing medial خ in بَخْت *(luck)*:

Now practice final خ by copying the word جَخ *(chic, fancy)*:

🎧 Drill 3. Recognizing ج , ح , and خ (At home)   12/12

There are twelve words, each containing ج , ح , or خ. Listen to each word on the audio, then select the letter you hear.

1. خ ح ج   2. خ ح ج   3. خ ح ج   4. خ ح ج

5. خ ح ج   6. خ ح ج   7. خ ح ج   8. خ ح ج

9. خ ح ج   10. خ ح ج   11. خ ح ج   12. خ ح ج

🎧 Drill 4. Letter connection (At home)

Connect the following letters to form words. Then listen to the words and write in the short vowels where you hear them:

1. خ + ا + ب + ت = _____ خابت

2. ح + ج + ا + ب = _____ حجاب

3. ح + ب + ي + ب = _____ حبيب

4. ت + و + خ + ت = <u>تخوت</u>

5. ب + و + ج + ت = <u>تجوب</u>

6. ث + و + ح + ب = <u>بحوث</u>

7. ي + ح + و + ب + ت = <u>تبوحي</u>

8. ت + ب + ج + ح = <u>حجبت / حجبت</u>

🎧 Drill 5. Dictation (At home)

Using the video, write below the words you hear, including all vowels. Watch and listen as many times as necessary.

1. <u>حجب</u>   2. <u></u>   3. <u>تنختي</u>

4. <u>حج</u>   5. <u>باحث</u>   6. <u>جبت</u>

🎧 Drill 6. Reading aloud (At-home preparation; in-class activation)

Read each of the following words aloud, paying special attention to vowel length and the sounds ح and خ. Then, check your pronunciation by listening to the audio.

9. حُب   1. تَحتاج تَحتَاج

10. باحِث   2. جابي جابي

11. تُجاب   3. حَج حَج

12. بُح   4. حِجاب

13. جيبوتي   5. جُبَب

14. تُخوت   6. حاج

15. خوجا   7. جابَت

8. خاب خاب

○
‾   **sukuun**

(handwritten annotation: ╱ = short "a", ‾ = short "e", ● = short "o")

This symbol is a pronunciation marker that occurs on consonants. The word sukuun means "silence", and a sukuun indicates the absence of a vowel following the consonant it is written on. So far, you have learned to use fatHa, Damma, and kasra over consonants to indicate short vowels, or ا , و , and ي to indicate long vowels. Consonants that are not followed by a vowel have been left "blank," such as تثبيت tathbiit, in which no vowel occurs between *th* and *b: tath-biit*. In fully vowelled texts, the absence of a vowel is marked so that all consonants have at least one marking. If no vowel follows the consonant, like *th* in *tathbiit*, a sukuun is written to indicate that the syllable ends there. After a medial sukuun, a new syllable begins, so a medial sukuun must be followed by a consonant.

To see how sukuun works, listen to and study the words shown below in Arabic script and in transliteration broken down syllable by syllable. Note that every syllable that ends in a consonant takes a sukuun, indicating that there is no vowel and hence no new syllable.

1. تَحْتَجْ (taH – taj)   2. تَخْتي (takh – tii)

3. تَحْجُبُ (taH – ju – bu)   4. تُثْبِتي (tuth – bi – tii)

5. بَحْثي (baH – thii)

🎧 Listening Exercise 4. Reading sukuun (At home)

Listen to the words you studied above and practice reading them by syllable.

🎧 Writing

○
‾

Like the short vowel symbols, the sukuun is rarely used in unvowelled or partially vowelled texts. When it is written, it appears as a small open circle above a letter not followed by a vowel. In writing sukuun, make sure to draw a closed circle and not a Damma or a dot. Practice writing sukuun in the words تَحْت *(below)*, تُبْت *(you repented)*, and بَخْتي *(my luck)*:

(handwritten practice: تَحْت   تُبْت)

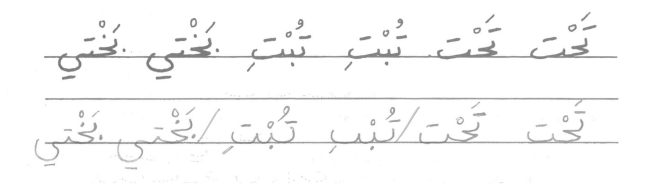

و waaw

In unit 2 you learned that the letter و represents the long vowel sound *uu*. It also has a second function related to the first one: When preceded or followed by a long or short vowel, this letter is pronounced *w* as in *well*, or as in the name of the letter: واو *waaw*. To see how these two sounds are related, pronounce *oo* and hold it *oooooooooo* then go right into *a*. You will hear a *w* sound connecting the two vowels. At the beginning of a word, و will always be pronounced *w* because Arabic words cannot begin with a vowel. **Remember**: any vowel, short or long, preceding or following و turns it into a consonant.

🎧 Listening Exercise 5. Pronouncing و (At home)

Listen to and repeat the words containing consonant و.

5. خَاوِي   4. حِوار   3. جَواب   2. واجِب   1. وَثَب

The letter و also represents the word وَ *and*, as in *ana wa anta* (formal), *you and I.*
You know that English *w* can occur with vowels in diphthongs, such as *ow* in *grow*. Similarly, Arabic و combines with fatHa to form the diphthong وَ (و preceded by a fatHa). In spoken Arabic this combination makes a sound similar to *ow* in *grow*. The sound of this diphthong in formal Arabic has no exact equivalent in English but falls somewhere in between *ow* in *grow* and *ow* in *now*. Listen to the examples and practice saying this sound aloud.

🎧 Listening Exercise 6. Hearing and pronouncing ـَوْ (At home)

Listen to the sound of the diphthong ـَوْ in these words and repeat:

1. ثَوْب   2. زَوْج   3. تَوْبِيخ   4. خَوْخ   5. حَوْل

In fully vowelled texts this diphthong is indicated with fatHa on the letter preceding و and sukuun on و , as you see in the words in Listening Exercise 6. In unvowelled texts the fatHa, or the sukuun, or both, may be omitted. Thus the following are all possible ways of writing the word *(peach)*:

خوخ   خْوخ   خَوخ   خَوْخ   خَوْخ

The sukuun alone (without fatHa on the previous letter) can indicate a diphthong because sukuun only occurs on consonants, so if you see ـوْ , you know that the و is functioning as a consonant and that a fatHa precedes it.

🎧 Drill 7. Dictation (At home)

Using the video, write below the words you hear, including all vowels. Watch and listen as many times as necessary.

1. _____ خَوْخ   2. _____ تَبْيِت تَكْتُبُها تَبْيِيتُ تَيْس

3. _____ جَوب   4. _____ ثَواب

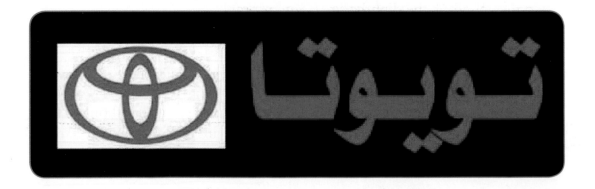

yaa

Like long vowel **و** , long vowel **ي** also functions as a consonant at the beginning of a word and whenever preceded by or followed by a vowel: it is pronounced like *y* in *yes*. Say *eeeee* and go right into *a* and you will hear yourself say *yaa*.

🎧 **Listening Exercise 7. Pronouncing ي (At home)**

Listen to words containing the consonant **ي** and repeat.

١. بُيُوت ٢. ثِياب ٣. جُيُوب ٤. يَجِب ٥. يَثوب

When **ي** is preceded by a fatHa and followed by sukuun, it forms a diphthong that is pronounced like *ay* as in *say* (it has a deeper sound following emphatic consonants). The sukuun alone may be written on **ي** to indicate this diphthong, or the fatHa may be used, or both sukuun and fatHa. Thus there are three different ways of vocalizing the word بيت *(house):*

بَيْت = بِيت = بَيْت

🎧 **Listening Exercise 8. Hearing and pronouncing ـَيْ (At home)**

Listen to the sound of the diphthong ـَيْ and repeat.

١. حَيْث ٢. خَيْر ٣. جَيْب ٤. بَيْت ٥. بَيْن

🎧 **Drill 8. Dictation (At home)**

Watch and listen to the video and write below the words you hear, including all vowels and sukuun. Watch as many times as necessary.

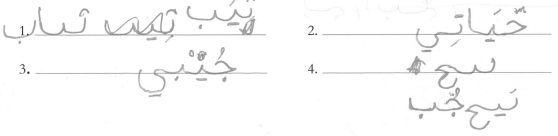

1. _____ ثَيْب تِـيـب نـاب

2. _____ حَيَاتِي

3. _____ جَيْبِي

4. _____ سـح نَـيحـجـب

🎧 Drill 9. Reading aloud (At-home preparation;
in-class activation)

Read each of the following words aloud. Then, check your pronunciation by listening to the audio.

15. تُجِيبـي	8. جَيـْبـي	١. ١ يَخْـت
16. خَابَ	9. جُيُـوب	٢. ثِيـابـي
17. يَجِـب	10. تَبـوحـي	٣. ٢ واجِبـات
18. جُثَث	11. ٦ بَحْـث	٤. حَبيـبـي
19. جَواب	12. بَيتـي	٥. ٣ حَبيـبَتـي
20. جَوابات	13. بُيُـوت	٦. ٤ حَيْـث
	14. وُجـوب	٧. ٧ ثَـواب

🎧 Drill 10. Letter connection (At home)

Connect the following letters to form words. Then listen to the words and write in the short vowels where you hear them:

1. ج + ا + ب + ت = ___ جَابِت ___
2. ح + ج + ب = حَجُب حَجُب ___
3. خ + و + خ = خَوخ ___
4. ث + ي + ا + ب + ي = ثِيابِـي ___
5. ج + ي + ب + و + ت + ي = جِيبُوتِي ___
6. ح + ب + ي + ب + ت + ي = حبيبـ حَبِيبَتِي ___
7. ب + ح + و + ث = بُحُوث ___

8. و + ا + ج + ا + ب + ا + ت = الواجبات

9. ب + ي + و + ت = بُيوت

10. ج + ي + و + ب = جُيوب

🎧 Drill 11. Dictation (At home)

Watch the video and write below the words you hear, including all vowels. Watch and listen as many times as necessary.

1. الواجب 2.  بَيتي 3.  يَبوح

4. يَاجِيب 5. يَحِجّ 6. تَحتَاج

يَحجُوب

Vocabulary and Conversation: Greeting People

Studying and Activating Vocabulary

In a few short weeks you will have mastered the Arabic alphabet and sound system. Learning vocabulary, on the other hand, is a process that takes much longer. Ultimately, your fluency in Arabic will depend more than anything else on the range and accuracy of your vocabulary. As the vocabulary lists accumulate, you will need to develop good strategies for active vocabulary acquisition. By "active" we mean that you have not really learned a word unless you can produce it as well as understand it in context.

The drills and exercises in this book that you do at home and in class are meant to help you in the process of activating vocabulary and to show you various strategies and activities that may be useful for you to do on your own. Studying or reviewing vocabulary should be part of your daily life, and it does not need to be done at a desk. We believe that the most efficient strategies for learning vocabulary are those that combine mechanical and creative activities in multiple modes. Notice, for example, that staring at the vocabulary chart is much less productive than reading, listening, and repeating the words aloud. Another good practice is to write the word five to ten times (in Arabic script as much as you can) and to pronounce words simultaneously.

The creative part of vocabulary work comes in the form of your own production, both speaking and writing. You will remember best the words that you "own," that have become part of your world. For every word you learn, think about what you can say with it that relates to your life. You talk with your classmates in class; at home you can talk to yourself, or the cat, the dog, or even the goldfish. Write to a real or imaginary person, to your classmate or teacher, or just to yourself. The important thing is that you create with the words you are learning. It does not matter if what you say is not entirely correct—accuracy will develop over time, and you will learn to monitor and correct yourself.

One final point to keep in mind is that you will not be able to express everything that you want to right now. Resist the temptation to ask for or look up extra new words, because this actually slows down your progression to fluency. It is important at this level to focus more on what you **can** say than what you **want** to say, and to try to say as much as you possibly can with words that you know now.

🎧 New Vocabulary (At home)

Listen to and learn the words in the vocabulary chart. You will find the masculine and feminine forms of "How are you?" separated by a slash, with the ending *-ak* indicating the masculine gender and *-ik* indicating the feminine gender. From now on, masculine and feminine forms of nouns and adjectives will be listed together, separated by a slash, with the masculine form preceding the feminine form.

Meaning	maSri	shaami	Formal /written
and	و	و	وَ
veil, head covering	حِجاب	حْجاب	حِجاب
house	بيت	بيت	بَيْت
street	شارِع shaari^c	شارِع shaari^c	شارِع shaari^c
homework	واجِب *Kitaab*	وَظيفة waZiife	واجِب *Kitaab*
news	أخْبار akhbaar	أخْبار akhbaar	أخْبار akhbaar
book	كِتاب kitaab	كتاب ktaab	كِتاب kitaab
my (male) dear, darling	حَبيبي	حَبيبي	حَبيبي
my (female) dear, darling	حَبيبتي	حَبيبتي	حَبيبَتي
Good morning!	صَباح الْخير SabaaH il-kheer	صَباح الْخير SabaaH il-kheer	صَباح الْخَير SabaaH al-khayr
(response to) Good morning!	صَباح النّور SabaaH in-nuur	صَباح النّور SabaaH in-nuur	صَباح النّور SabaaH an-nuur
signal that you are addressing someone directly	يا ...	يا ...	يا ...

Meaning	maSri		shaami		Formal /written	
How?	izzayy?	إِزَّيّ؟	kiif?	كيف؟	kayfa?	كَيْفَ؟
How are you? (masc./ fem.)	izzayyak/–ik?	إِزَّيّك؟	kiifak/–ik?	كيفك؟	kayfa al-Haal?	كَيْفَ الحال؟
(response to) How are you?	il-Hamdu lillaah	الْحَمدُ لله	il-Hamdilla	الْحَمد لِله	al-Hamdu lillaah	الْحَمدُ لِله
great, fine	tamaam	تَمام	tamaam	تَمام	jayyid jayyida	جَيِّد جَيِّدة
OK	maashi	ماشي	maashi	ماشي	-	
this (masc.)	da	دا	haada hayda	هادا، هَيدا	haadhaa	هٰذا
this (fem.)	di	دي	haadi haydi	هادي، هَيدي	haadhihi	هٰذِهِ
good (masc.) good (fem.)	kuwayyis kuwayyisa	كوَيِّس كوَيِّسة	mniiH mniiHa	منيح منيحة	bi-khayr (reply to kayfa al-Haal?)	بِخَير
(am/are/is) not	mish	مِش	muu	مو	laysa	لَيْسَ

The words حَبيبي and حَبيبتي can be used with anyone you love, including children, parents, and close friends.

🎧 Drill 12. Vocabulary matching (At home)

This exercise is found at www.alkitaabtextbook.com only. Listen to the vocabulary words and match them to the corresponding picture.

Drill 13. Vocabulary practice (At-home preparation; in-class activation)

Ask your classmates questions with new and old vocabulary and answer their questions. Greet them first, introduce yourself if you have not worked with them before, and ask them how they are. Remember to think about the gender of the person you are talking to. Questions you can ask include:

Where is your house?

Where is your book?

Where is your homework?

What is your news?

When you have gotten all the information you can from the first person, find a new partner and repeat.

🎧 **Drill 14. Listen and interact (At home)**

Listen to the scene on the audio where you encounter someone you know who will initiate a conversation with you. Reply out loud, greet him or her, and respond to the person's questions using as much Arabic as you can.

🎧 **Drill 15. Scene 3A: *izzay Hadritik?/kiifik?* and Scene 3B: *SabaaH l-Kheer* (At-home preparation; in-class activation)**

Watch scenes 3A and 3B in these steps:

1. First listen: What are the two people doing? Do they know each other? How do you know?
2. Second listen: What words and expressions do you hear this time?
3. Third listen: Before listening a third time, prepare your questions.
    What parts of the exchange do you want to understand more of?
    What do you think is happening in that section?
    Based on this hypothesis, what words and expressions do you expect to hear?
    Write down what you think was said.
4. In class, discuss the scenes with your classmates and go over any questions.
    Listen once more to prepare for activation, then have a "reception" in which you arrive one by one and mingle, greet and ask about each other. *ahlan!*

Culture: Expressions *SabaaH il-khayr!* and *al-Hamdu li-llaah!*

In Arab culture it is considered rude not to say good morning, good evening, or hello to people you know, even casually, the first time you see them each day. Handshaking is not usually a daily practice but is used whenever one wants to convey a warm greeting, no matter what the reason. Same-gender kissing on the cheeks (once on each cheek in most places, but local practices vary) is another greeting practice you will see and experience, especially in the context of welcoming someone. It is a sign of warmth, welcome, and respect within the parameters of the extended family and in circles of good friends. Close friends of the same gender kiss each other on the cheeks if they have not seen each other for a while, or if one has returned from a trip, or on any special occasion where extra warmth is warranted.

Literally *Praise Be to God, Thank God*, al-Hamdu li-llaah is one of the most widely used phrases in Arabic by people of all religious backgrounds. Its most common uses are (a) in response to *How are you?* whether or not one is well, because God is to be thanked at all times; (b) upon finishing a meal, to signal that one has had enough; and (c) upon successfully completing a task or learning of a positive outcome.

الوحدة الرابعة
Unit Four

In this unit:

The consonant hamza ء أ

Numbers 0–10

Letters د ذ ر ز

Culture: Introducing Someone

Culture: Forms of Address

Letters and Sounds: Part One

In this unit you will learn about the second function of alif and the next four consonants in the alphabet. All of these consonants are nonconnectors, that is, they do not connect to a following letter. You will also learn how to say and write the numerals 0–10, and practice introducing people to others.

ء hamza

In unit 3 you learned that و and ي sometimes function as consonants, representing the sounds *w* and *y*. They function this way whenever they are at the beginning of a word, as in the words واجب and يا . You have also learned several words that begin with vowel sounds, such as *ism* and *akhbaar*. But you also know that a short vowel cannot be written on its own, it must be written on a consonant. To write *ism*, we cannot use ي because that would result in a *y* sound: *yism*. This problem is solved with a consonant called hamza.

Hamza is not a vowel but rather, like other consonants, it is a carrier of vowel sounds. It is a sound you make in English all the time—every time you say a word that begins with a vowel, in fact—but you do not recognize it as a consonant because English has no letter for it. In linguistic terminology, this sound is called a glottal stop. Say *uh-oh* several times and pay attention to the sound you make in between the two syllables. You make the same sound when you pronounce any word that begins with a vowel, such as *our, if, it, I, on, up*. Say these words out loud and pay attention to the "catch" in your throat as you pronounce the first vowel. This sound is not written in English, which treats these words as if they began with a vowel. In Arabic, however, this sound is considered to be a consonant. **Remember:** in Arabic, no word or syllable begins with a vowel. What sounds to English speakers like an Arabic word that begins with a vowel is actually a word that begins with hamza.

For historic reasons that involve Qur'anic spelling, hamza has no place of its own in the alphabet. Tradition holds that the dialect of Mecca, which the Prophet Muhammed spoke, did not have this sound, therefore it was not written when the Qur'an was first recorded in script. The symbol for the hamza was developed, along with the short vowel markings, at a later date. This is why hamza has several different "spellings," depending on its position in the word and the vowel sounds surrounding it.

In this unit you will learn two common spellings, أ and ء. We will present the other spellings in unit 8. In most transliteration systems, including ours, hamza is represented by an apostrophe: '.

When a word begins with hamza, it is always written on an alif "seat." In everyday print and handwriting, initial hamza is usually written on top of the alif that "carries" or represents it. Thus, initial hamza may appear as ‏ا‎ or as ‏أ‎ . The combination ‏أ‎ is called alif-hamza. **Remember**: Alif at the beginning of a word is always a seat for hamza, never a long vowel. Since hamza is a consonant, it takes a vowel or sukuun. You will see and hear examples of alif-hamza with fatHa in Listening Exercise 1.

🎧 **Listening Exercise 1. Listening to and pronouncing hamza (At home)**

Practice saying ‏ء‎ by listening to and repeating the words.

1. ‏أَخْوات‎   2. ‏أَب‎   3. ‏سَبَأ‎   4. ‏تَأَتَأ‎   5. ‏بَأس‎

🎧 **Drill 1. Recognizing hamza (At home)**

Listen to the audio to hear a selection of twelve words. For each, select Yes if you hear hamza and select No if you do not. Remember to listen at the beginning and end of the word as well as in the middle.

1. **Yes** No	2. **Yes** No	3. **Yes** No	4. **Yes** No
5. **Yes** No	6. **Yes** No	7. **Yes** No	8. **Yes** No
9. **Yes** No	10. **Yes** No	11. **Yes** No	12. **Yes** No

🎧 **Listening Exercise 2. Listening to initial hamza with fatHa (At home)**

Listen to initial hamza with fatHa ‏أ‎ in these words and read along with the audio.

1. ‏أَب‎   2. ‏أَتَت‎   3. ‏أَخ‎   4. ‏أَخَوات‎   5. ‏أثاث‎

At the beginning of a word, hamza is represented by alif, either ‏ا‎ or ‏أ‎ . However, the vowel sound this alif-hamza represents may be any of the short vowels: fatHa, Damma, or kasra. The words in Listening Exercise 2 all begin with hamza followed by the vowel fatHa. In other cases, the other short vowels may appear in this position; that is, ‏أ‎ serves as a seat for Damma and kasra as well as for fatHa. When the initial vowel is kasra, the hamza is often written underneath the alif, as in: ‏إتبات‎. **Remember**: While ‏أ‎ can carry the kasra, hamza underneath the alif ‏إ‎ always indicates a kasra vowel. Listen to examples of Damma and kasra on alif-hamza in Listening Exercise 3 and read along.

🎧 Listening Exercise 3. Initial hamza with Damma and kasra (At home)

Listen to initial hamza with vowels Damma and kasra and repeat.

3. إِثْبات   2. أُخْت   1. إِبْحار

6. أُثْبِتَ   5. إِخْبار   4. أُخْرِجَ

In fully vocalized texts the short vowel will be marked. In unvocalized texts you will see only the consonant skeleton. Here, as elsewhere, to read an unvocalized word correctly, you need to know it, or make an educated guess based on knowledge of Arabic word patterns (this will become clear later on). Learn to associate the

pronunciation of each new vocabulary item with its consonant frame the same way you associate certain pronunciations in English with certain spellings (think of *neighbor* and *weigh, taught* and *caught*). In your native language you read by word, not by syllable, and it is important to develop this same skill in Arabic.

🎧 Writing

ء   أ

The actual shape of the hamza, shown above, is a small "c" shape that continues into a line on the bottom. Watch Professor El-Shinnawi write the hamza, first on the line and then on alif, and practice with him. At the beginning of a word it is always written on alif (where the hamza itself is sometimes omitted in unvowelled texts, leaving the alif to represent it). When hamza occurs in the middle of a word, it may be written on a seat that has the shape of any of the long vowels: أ , ؤ, or ئ (you will learn more about these spellings of hamza in unit 8). When hamza occurs after a long vowel at the end of a word, it is written on the line, without a seat, in which case it is a bit larger in size. Copy and practice the shape of independent hamza:

ع ع ءِ ①

ء ء ء ء ء ء ء ء ء ء ء ء ء

🎧 **Listening Exercise 4. Final hamza (At home)**

The names of many letters of the alphabet end in hamza. Listen to and repeat the names of letters you have learned.

5. خاء   4. حاء   3. ثاء   2. تاء   1. باء

Practice writing and pronouncing final hamza by copying the names of these letters:

باء باء تاء تاء ثاء ثاء حاء حاء خاء خاء

باء باء تاء تاء ثاء حاء خاء خاء

باء باء تاء تاء ثاء حاء خاء خاء

Practice writing initial hamza on alif by copying أخ *(brother)*, أُخت *(sister)*, and
إثبات *(proof)*:

أخ أخ أُخت أُخت إثبات إثبات

أخ أخ أُخت أُخت إثبا إثبات

أخ أخ أُخت أُخت إثبا إثبات

🎧 **Drill 2. Dictation (At home)**

013-55 66791

Watch and listen to the video, and write below the words you hear, including all vowels. Watch and listen as many times as necessary.

1. _____Yes_____   2. _____no_____   3. _____yes_____

4. _____no_____   5. _____yes_____   6. _____no_____

🎧 **Drill 3. Distinguishing initial hamza, و, and ي (At home)**

Listen to the audio to hear six words that begin with hamza followed by a vowel, or with one of the consonants و or ي. Select the letter that represents the sound you hear.

1. أ   إ   و   ي   2. أ   إ   و   ي

3. أ   إ   و   ي   4. أ   إ   و   ي

5. أ   إ   و   ي   6. أ   إ   و   ي

05923761   2027669143
7038569421
707243695
6789243090
4162900874
04469 48015
010768 1705
944304 07667

Arabic Numerals and Numbers

Two related sets of numerals, shown in the chart, are used in the Arab world. The second column from the left, "Arabic–Indic Numerals," contains the set that was developed first, in the eastern part of the Arab world. The numerals in the leftmost column were developed in North Africa and were introduced into Europe from Islamic Spain in the Middle Ages—hence our name for them, Arabic numerals. The use of these numerals has recently been spreading across the eastern Arab world through print media and other technologies. Arab and Muslim mathematicians adopted their numerals from India and expanded on earlier Hindu and Greek contributions to develop algebra and other branches of higher mathematics.

🎧 Numbers 0–10 (At home)

Listen to and learn the Arabic names for these numerals:

Arabic Numerals	Arabic–Indic Numerals	maSri		shaami		Formal / written	
0	٠	Sifr ziiru	صِفر زيرو	Sifər	صِفر	Sifr	صِفْر
1	١	waaHid	واحِد	waaHid	واحِد	waaHid	واحِد
2	٢	itneen	إِتنين	tneen	اتنين	ithnayn	إِثنَين
3	٣	talaata	تَلاتة	tlaate	تلاتة	thalaatha	ثَلاثة
4	٤	arbᶜa	اربعة	arbᶜa	اربعة	arbaᶜa	أَربَعة
5	٥	khamsa	خمسة	khamse	خمسة	khamsa	خَمسة
6	٦	sitta	سِتّة	sitte	سِتّة	sitta	سِتّة
7	٧	sabᶜa	سَبعة	sabᶜa	سَبعة	sabᶜa	سَبعة
8	٨	tamanya	تَمانية	tmaane	تمانية	thamaaniya	ثَمانية
9	٩	tisᶜa	تِسعة	tisᶜa	تِسعة	tisᶜa	تِسعة
10	١٠	ᶜashara	عَشَرة	ᶜashra	عَشَرة	ᶜashara	عَشَرة

🎧 Writing

Watch Professor El-Shinnawi write the numbers 0–10. Notice that he writes zero as a dot, and pay attention to the way he writes the numerals 2 and 3. The handwritten shapes of these two numerals look different than their print forms, and it is important to learn the different shapes so that you do not misunderstand, or be misunderstood. In print, ٢ and ٣ appear in these shapes. In handwriting, however, they take on slightly different forms, in which the handwritten 3 resembles a printed 2, except that its "dip" is much deeper. Following Ustaaz El-Shinnawi and the examples below, practice writing these two numerals:

= ٣   = ٢

You can see that the numeral ٢ in print closely resembles the numeral ٣ when written by hand, except that the hook at the top of handwritten ٢ is usually deeper. To avoid confusion, always write these numerals as shown in the handwritten example above, and when reading, remember to differentiate between printed and handwritten forms.

١٠ ٩ ٨ ٧ ٦ ٥ ٤ ٣ ٢ ١

١٠ ٩ ٨ ٧ ٦ ٥ ٤ ٣ ٢ ١٠

١٠ ٩ ٨ ٧ ٦ ٥ ٤ ٣ ٢ ٢ ١٠

Writing Numbers Greater than 9

Numbers in Arabic are not written from right to left but rather from left to right, just like numbers in English. The reason for this is that Arabic numbers were traditionally read from right to left in the same direction they are written: ones, then tens, then hundreds, and so on. Only recently have larger numbers (hundreds and above) come to be read before ones and tens.

Compare the following English and Arabic equivalents of various numbers. Note that Arabic uses a comma rather than a period for the decimal point, and does not normally mark commas in large numbers or hyphens in telephone numbers.

٢,٥٠ = 2.50   ١٠٧٨٩ = 10,789

٥٦٩٠٨٩٤ = 569-0894   ١٩٥٥ = 1955

٣٢٥ = 325

Now practice writing large numbers by writing out your telephone number, left to right:

٦٥٧–٣٤٦–١٣١٥

and your birth date: first day, then month, then year, separated by hyphens or slashes:

١٠/٢٨/‎١٩٩٦

Vocabulary and Conversation: Introductions

🎧 New Vocabulary 1 (At home)

In this vocabulary section you will find masculine and feminine nouns referring to people. How do they differ? In Arabic, nouns referring to human beings reflect the natural gender of the person. All other nouns are either masculine or feminine, which means there is no ungendered word for *it* in Arabic, and the words huwa *(huwwa, huwwe)* or *hiya (hiyya, hiyye)* refer to both human and nonhuman nouns. Remember that you will see words whose letters you know only in Arabic script, without transliteration. You should put this into practice too: From now on, stop using transliteration for all the words whose letters you know. Listen to and learn these expressions.

Meaning	maSri		shaami		Formal /written	
please come in, go ahead (to a male)	itfaDDal	اِتفَضَّل	tfaDDal	تفَضَّل	tafaDDal	تَفَضَّل
please come in, go ahead (to a female)	itfaDDali	اِتفَضَّلي	tfaDDli	تفَضَّلي	tafaDDalii	تَفَضَّلي
please come in, go ahead (plural)	itfaDDalu	اِتفَضَّلوا	tfaDDlu	تفَضَّلوا	tafaDDaluu	تَفَضَّلوا
my (male) friend; my boyfriend	SaHbi	صاحبي	SaaHbi rfii'i	صاحبي رفيقي	SaaHibii	صاحِبي
my (female) friend; my girlfriend	SaHbiti	صاحبتي	SaaHibti rfii'ti	صاحِبتي رفيقتي	SaaHibatii	صاحِبَتي
he/it (masc.)	huwwa	هو	huwwe	هو	huwa	هُوَ
she/it (fem.)	hiyya	هي	hiyye	هي	hiya	هِيَ

Meaning	maSri		shaami		Formal /written	
his	–u	ـُه	–o	ـُه	–hu	ـُه
his name	ismu	اسمُه	ismo	اسمُه	ismuhu	اسمُهُ
her / hers	–ha	ـها	–a	ـها	–ha	ـها
her name	ismaha	اسمها	isma	اسمها	ismuha	اسمُها
student (male)	Taalib	طالِب	Taalib	طالِب	Taalib	طالِب
student (female)	Taaliba	طالبة	Taalbe	طالبة	Taaliba	طالبة
professor, teacher (male)	ustaaz	أُستاذ	istaaz	إِستاذ	ustaadh	أُسْتاذ
professor, teacher (female)	ustaaza	أُستاذة	istaaze	إِستاذة	ustaadha	أُستاذة
the university of...	gamᶜit ...	جامعة	jaamᶜit ...	جامعة	jaamiᶜat ...	جامِعة

🎧 Drill 4. Scene 4A: *izayyak?/kiifak?* and
Scene 4B: *al-Hamdu Lillah/l-Hamdilla*
(At-home preparation; in-class activation)

After you have studied the expressions in New Vocabulary 1, watch scenes 4A and 4B.

1. First listen: What is the situation? Do these people know each other? What are they doing?
2. Second listen: What new and old expressions do you recognize?
3. Third listen: Before listening, focus your attention on the parts you want to understand better. What do you want to learn this time?
4. In class: After discussing the scenes with your classmates and teacher, listen once more for final details and prepare to use what you have heard to introduce your classmates to each other.

Culture: Introducing Someone

In English we often use the phrase *this is* to introduce people, as in *This is my friend Tom*, or *This is my sister Dina*. In Arabic, however, we usually avoid using *this is* to refer to people. To introduce someone, just say the person's name and her or his relationship to you, as you heard in scenes 4A and 4B.

Drill 5. Vocabulary practice (At-home preparation; in-class activation)

(A) Write five sentences about your friends using as much of the new vocabulary as you can.

Example: SaHbi Cory Taalib fi gam3it Colorado.

Remember to say the sentences out loud as you write them.

(B) Using your new vocabulary and the expressions you heard in scenes 4A and 4B, prepare to introduce your classmates to each other. Rehearse before class so you are ready to speak and interact during class.

>> Letters and Sounds: Part Two

د daal

This consonant is pronounced like a clear, frontal *d* in English, as in the word *deep* (not like the *d* sound in *puddle*). Pay particular attention to your pronunciation of medial and final د , which should retain the same frontal position, and to the surrounding vowel sounds, which should be frontal in quality (like *e* in *bet*).

🎧 Listening Exercise 5. Recognizing and pronouncing د (At home)

Listen to and read aloud the words containing د.

١. دَجاج   ٢. خُدود   ٣. حُدود

٤. جَديد   ٥. أَدَب   ٦. أَحداث

🎧 Writing

د   ـد   د   ـد

Like alif, the letter د does not connect to any letter that follows it. Watch Ustaaz El-Shinnawi and imitate the shape he draws. To write initial د, begin well above the line and slant down as shown below. Just before reaching the line, angle sharply and finish along the line. In handwriting, the exact shape and slant of this letter vary slightly according to individual style, but it is important to keep the angle of the body of this letter **less** than 90 degrees and to keep it **above** the line. Copy the examples:

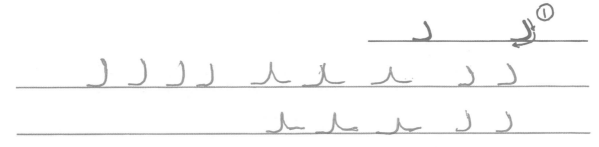

To write د when it is connected to a previous letter in medial or final position, begin from the connecting segment, draw the top half of the letter from the line up, then trace your line back down, make a sharp angle as before, and finish. When connected from the previous letter, the top half of the angle tends to have a slightly different shape because of the connecting segment. Copy:

Now practice by copying the words دَجاج *(chicken)* and جَديد *(new)*:

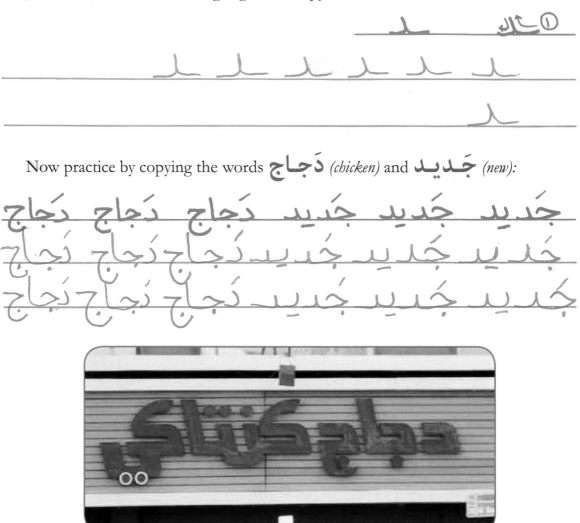

ذ dhaal

In unit 1 you learned to distinguish between the sound *th* in *three*, represented in Arabic by the letter ث , and the sound *th* in the word *other*. The letter ذ represents the *other* sound (pun intended; remember it this way!). Practice hearing and pronouncing this distinction in Listening Exercise 6 and Drill 7.

🎧 Listening Exercise 6. Reading and pronouncing ذ (At home)

Listen to words containing ذ and read aloud.

١. ذُباب   ٢. ذات   ٣. بَذَرَ

٤. خُذ   ٥. حَذارِ   ٦. تَذَبْذُب

🎧 Drill 6. Pronouncing ث and ذ (At home)

Read the following words aloud with the audio, paying particular attention to the pronunciation of ث and ذ.

١. ذابَ   ٢. ثابَ   ٣. ذُباب   ٤. ثَبات

٥. ثَواب   ٦. ذَوات   ٧. جُثَث   ٨. جاذِب

🎧 Drill 7. Distinguishing between ث and ذ (At home)

Listen to the audio to hear the twelve words that follow each containing either ذ or ث. Select the letter that corresponds to the sound you hear in each word.

1. ث ذ   2. ث ذ   3. ث ذ   4. ث ذ

5. ث ذ   6. ث ذ   7. ث ذ   8. ث ذ

9. ث ذ   10. ث ذ   11. ث ذ   12. ث ذ

🎧 Writing

ذ   ذ   ـذ   ـذ

The letter ذ is written just like د, except that it takes a single dot above. Like د, it does not connect to a following letter, and so has only two forms, initial/independent and medial/final. Watch Ustaaz El-Shinnawi write this letter in its connected and unconnected forms. Practice the initial/independent form by copying ذُباب *(flies)*:

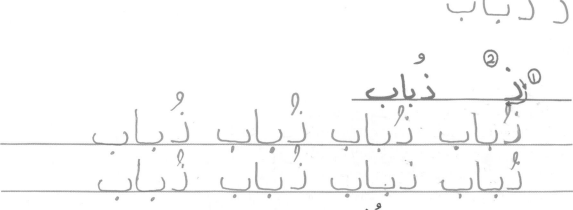

ز ذ ذُباب

Practice writing the medial/final form by copying خُذ *(take!)*:

Now copy and read aloud these words:

ذات (self)   يَذوب (it melts)   أَخَذْتُ (I took)

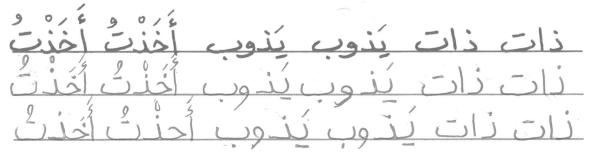

🎧 **Drill 8. Reviewing the difference between ث and ذ (At home)**

Listen to the audio to hear words containing either ث or ذ and select which letter corresponds to the sound you hear in each word.

١. تَ ..... وب   ٢. خُوَ .....   ٣. ..... ات

٤. أ ..... واب   ٥. ..... وبي   ٦. جَ ..... ب

٧. أ ..... ا   ٨. خُ ..... ي

ر raa

This is the name of the Arabic *r*. It is a flap, like the Spanish or Italian *r*. You already know how to make this sound: it is the sound American English speakers make when they say *gotta* as in *gotta go*. Say *gotta* several times in a row very quickly and pay attention to what your tongue is doing. You should feel it flapping against the roof of your mouth behind your teeth. Now pronounce the sound alone. Another good exercise is

to practice making a whirring sound: *rrrrrrrrrr*. Practice these exercises daily until you have mastered this sound, and go back to the alphabet chart in the Introduction to watch it being pronounced.

🎧 Listening Exercise 7. Pronouncing ر (At home)

Listen to and read aloud words containing ر. Note that ر often deepens the quality of alif and fatHa so that they sound like *a* in *father*.

٣. خَراج	٢. رُدود	١. رَبـاب
٦. وُرود	٥. جار	٤. تَبْرير

🎧 Writing

ر   ر   ـر   ـر

This letter is a nonconnector and is written almost entirely below the line. Watch Ustaaz El-Shinnawi and copy his example. You will see that the exact angle and shape of the ر vary somewhat in handwriting and print styles, but it is distinguished from د by its wide angle and its long body that rests **below** the line (as opposed to the sharp angle of د, which rests on **top** of the line). To write initial ر, begin on the line and curve downwards below it. Imitate the shape in the example:

To write ـر connected from a previous letter, start from the connecting segment on the line, then curve down. Do **not** go upwards above the line to make a "tooth" at the beginning but rather drop immediately down from the line. Copy:

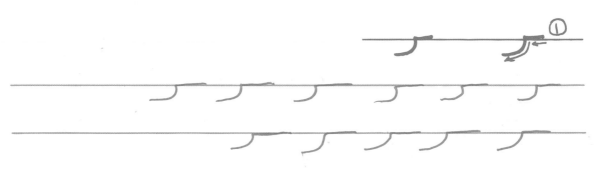

ز zaay

This consonant corresponds to the English sound *z* in *zebra*.

🎧 **Listening Exercise 8. Pronouncing ز (At home)**

Listen to and read aloud words containing the sound ز.

٣. زُجاج	٢. أَحْـزاب	١. زَوْج
٦. تَـزيد	٥. جَواز	٤. يَـزور

🎧 Writing

ز ـز ـز

The letter ز is a nonconnector and has the same shape as ر, except that it takes one dot above. Watch and imitate Ustaaz El-Shinnawi write ز in its connecting and nonconnecting forms. Practice writing initial/independent ز by copying the word زَوج *(husband)*:

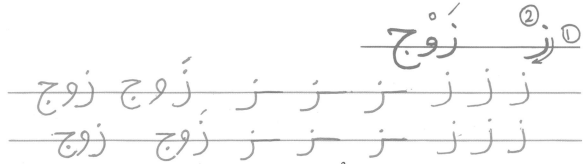

Copy ـز in medial/final position in the word خُبز *(bread)*:

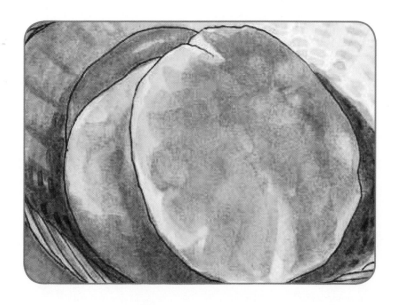

🎧 **Drill 9. Letter connection (At home)**

Connect the letters to form words. Then listen to them and write in the short vowels you hear:

١. ذ + ا + ذ + ر = <u>رَذَاذ</u>

٢. ر + د + ا + خ = <u>خَادِر</u>

٣. د + ر + ز = <u>زُرْد</u>

٤. ب + و + ر + ح = _____

٥. ء + ا + ج + ر = _____

٦. ر + ا + ح + ب = _____

٧. ج + ا + و + ز + أ = _____

٨. د + و + د + ح = _____

٩. د + و + د + ر = _____

١٠. ر ي + ذ + ح + ت = _____

١١. ر + ا + و + د + أ = _____

١٢. ج + ر + خ + ي = _____

١٣. ب + ر + ا + ج + ت = _____

١٤. ت + ح + ب + ذ = _____

🎧 **Drill 10. Dictation (At home)**

Using the video, write below the words you see and hear, including all vowels. Watch and listen as many times as necessary.

١. _____

٢. _____

٣. _____

٤. _____

٥. _____

٦. _____

٧. _____

٨. _____

٩. _____

١٠. _____

Drill 11. Reading aloud (In class)

(A)   Read the following words aloud.

(B)   After you have read through the list, go back and review the list to look for pairs of words that share three consonants in the same order (they will be adjacent to or near each other). What are the shared consonants in each case?

٢٥. جَريـر	١٧. دَجاج	٩. زَيْت	١. دار
٢٦. أَحزاب	١٨. أَجري	١٠. أَبـي	٢. واحِد
٢٧. دَيْر	١٩. حَرب	١١. بِحار	٣. وَحيـد
٢٨. وَزير	٢٠. يَجري	١٢. وَباء	٤. وَرْد
٢٩. أَخَوات	٢١. أُخْت	١٣. زُجاج	٥. زُيـوت
٣٠. ثَور	٢٢. حِزْب	١٤. خَبَـر	٦. أزرار
٣١. وُزَراء	٢٣. حُروب	١٥. أَخْبـار	٧. يُبحِر
٣٢. بارِد	٢٤. يَدور	١٦. تَحْذيـر	٨. ذَوات

>> Vocabulary and Conversation: More Introductions

 New Vocabulary 2 (At home)

Listen to and learn these words. For class, think about and be ready to talk about what you can say in Arabic, such as the things you have and the people you like.

Meaning	maSri		shaami		Formal /written	
bread	^ceesh	عيش		خُبز		خُبز
chicken	firaakh	فِراخ		دجاج		دَجاج
neighbor (male)		جار		جار		جار
neighbor (female)	gaara	جارة	jaara	جارة	jaara	جارة
brother		أَخ		أَخ		أَخ
sister		أُخت		أُخت		أُخت
new (masc.)		جِديد		جديد		جَديد
new (fem.)	gidiida	جِديدة	jdiide	جديدة	jadiida	جَديدة
Good evening!	misaa' il-kheer	مساء الخير	masa l-kheer	مسا الخير	masaa' al-khayr	مَساء الخَير
(response to) Good evening!	misaa' in-nuur	مساء النّور	masa n-nuur	مسا النّور	masaa' an-nuur	مَساء النّور
I have	^candi	عندي	^candi	عندي	^cindi	عِندي
I don't have	ma ^candiish	ما عنديش	maa ^candi	ما عندي	laysa ^cindi	لَيسَ عِندي
question	su'aal	سُؤال	su'aal	سُؤال	su'aal	سُؤال
I love		باحِبّ		بحِبّ		أُحِبّ
you (masc.) love		بِتحِبّ		بِتحِبّ		تُحِبّ
you (fem.) love		بِتحِبّي		بِتحِبّي	tuHibbiin	تُحِبّين
telephone number	nimrit tilifuun	نِمرة تليفون	nimrit tilifuun	نِمرة تليفون	raqm tilifuun	رَقم تِليفون

Drill 12. Vocabulary activation (At home)

Write as many sentences as it takes for you to use all the new vocabulary from New Vocabulary 2.

🎧 Drill 13. Dialing the telephone (At home)

This exercise is available on the companion website only. Complete it by following this scenario: You heard a contest on the radio to "call in and win." The telephone numbers will be announced by digit. "Dial" these numbers by clicking each one on your screen. If you dial correctly, the phone will start ringing!

Drill 14. Exchanging telephone numbers. (At-home preparation; in-class activation)

Prepare for this activity by memorizing your telephone number in Arabic numerals. In class, get the names and phone numbers of your classmates—in Arabic—and write them in your notebook.

🎧 Drill 15. Vocabulary matching (At home)

This exercise is available on the companion website only. Practice recognizing new vocabulary in context by matching the phrases you hear with the pictures shown on the screen.

Drill 16. Vocabulary practice (In class)

With a partner, use new and old vocabulary and your imagination to talk about this picture:

🎧 **Drill 17. Listen and interact (At home)**

Listening to the audio for this exercise, you will hear someone who you do not know very well initiate a conversation with you. Find out more about each other using as much Arabic as you can.

🎧 **Drill 18. Scene 4C:** *tasharrafna / tsharrafna* **(At-home preparation; in-class activation)**

After you have studied the vocabulary and expressions in New Vocabulary 2, watch scene 4C.

1. First listen: What is the situation? Who are the people in this scene?
2. Second listen: How does this situation differ from the last scenes you watched? What new and old expressions do you recognize?
3. Third listen: Before listening, focus your attention on the parts you want to under stand better. What do you want to learn this time?
4. In class: After discussing the scenes with your classmates and teacher, listen again for final details and prepare to use what you have heard. In groups of three, think of a formal introduction situation and practice what you would say.

Culture: Forms of Address

In addition to the polite "you" forms HaDritak (حَضْرِتَك) and HaDritik (حَضْرِتِك), titles are also used to address people politely. Some of the most common titles are:

used to address or refer to medical and academic professionals	duktuur duktuura	دُكتور دُكتورة
used to address or refer to an educated person, white-collar employee, school teacher, etc.	ustaadh or ustaaz ustaadha or ustaaza	أُستـاذ أُستـاذة
used in very formal situations and correspondence to refer to or introduce people who have no professional title	sayyid sayyida	سَيِّد سَيِّدة
used to address or refer to an older and/or married woman	madaam	مَدام
used to address or refer to a young, unmarried woman	aanisa	آنِسـة

These titles are traditionally followed by the person's **first** or **full** name (not by the last name alone). When used to address someone directly, these titles may be preceded by يا : yaa duktuur George; yaa duktuura Zeinab; yaa ustaaz Muhammad; yaa aanisa Khadija.

الوحدة الخامسة
Unit Five

In this unit:

Doubled consonants with shadda ـّ

Letters س ش ص ض

Culture: Good-bye!

Vocabulary and Conversation: Being Polite

Uses of itfaDDal اتفضّل

Roots

>> Letters and Sounds: Part One

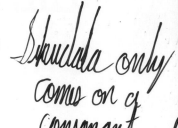

ــّ shadda

Shadda is a pronunciation marker whose function is to double the length of a consonant in pronunciation. This doubling also affects the meaning of words in Arabic. In English, we spell many words with doubled consonants, such as *little* and *recommend*, but we do not pronounce the *t* and *m* in these words that are doubled in length, and the spelling has no effect on the meaning of the word. (Doubling in English often indicates a difference in the prononciaton of the previous vowel: if *little* were spelled with one *t*, we would pronounce it like *title*.) **Remember:** In Arabic, doubling changes both the **pronunciation** of the consonant on which it is written and the **meaning** of the word in which it occurs. Like other vocalization marks, shadda is usually omitted in unvowelled texts, except in rare cases where ambiguity might arise without it.

Any medial or final consonant may be doubled, but the first consonant in a word is never doubled. The difference between a single consonant and a doubled one is length: A doubled consonant is pronounced and held for twice as long as a single one. This is easy to do with fluid sounds like ز , ث , ذ , ج , ح , خ , ر , and ز . To double the sounds ت , ب , and د , begin to say them and pause in the middle of pronouncing them for a second. Practice this along with the voice in Listening Exercise 1. Another key to hearing and pronouncing shadda is word stress. A syllable that has shadda at the end of it will always carry the stress or accent in the word. You will hear this contrast in the first pair of words in the next exercise.

🎧 Listening Exercise 1. Hearing and pronouncing shadda (At home)

The following pairs of words contrast consonants with and without shadda. Listen to the pairs of words and repeat them aloud several times until you can hear and pronounce the difference in each case. In each pair the shadda makes a difference in meaning.

٣. حاجة / حاجّة ٢. دَرَسَ / دَرَّسَ ١. تَجِدُ / تَجِدُّ

٥. خَرَجَ / خَرَّج ٤. شاب / شابّ

[handwritten note: Shudda only comes on a consonant and it doubles it.]

🎧 Drill 1. Identifying shadda (At home)

Listen to the twelve words on the audio. For each, select Yes if you hear shadda and No if you do not.

1. Yes No   2. Yes No   3. Yes No   4. Yes No

5. Yes No   6. Yes No   7. Yes No   8. Yes No

9. Yes No   10. Yes No   11. Yes No   12. Yes No

Distinguishing between a consonant doubled with a shadda and a long vowel sound requires practice and repetition. Remember that و and ي can be both consonants and vowels. When these letters function as consonants, giving a *w* and *y* sound, respectively, they can take a shadda. You will hear examples of this in Listening Exercise 2. Practice making this distinction, and keep working on the pronunciation of both shadda and long vowels as you learn new vocabulary.

🎧 Listening Exercise 2. Contrasting shadda and long vowels (At home)

Listen to the following pairs of words. The first word has a long vowel and the second word has a shadda. Listen and repeat aloud until you can hear and say the difference.

٣. تَزاوَجَ / تَزَوَّجَ   ٢. جاوَزَ / جَوَّزَ   ١. راجَعَ / رَجَّعَ

٥. دوري / دُرّي   ٤. دارِس / دَرِّس

🎧 Drill 2. Identifying shadda and long vowels (At home)

Listen to the twelve words on the video. Each contain either shadda or a long vowel. Select the letter that represents the sound you hear.

1.   ـّ   ا   و   ي   2.   ـّ   ا   و   ي

3.   ـّ   ا   و   ي   4.   ـّ   ا   و   ي

5.   ـّ   ا   و   ي   6.   ـّ   ا   و   ي

7.   ـّ   ا   و   ي   8.   ـّ   ا   و   ي

9.   ـّ   ا   و   ي   10.   ـّ   ا   و   ي

11.   ـّ   ا   و   ي   12.   ـّ   ا   و   ي

 Writing

Shadda is written like a tiny, rounded *w* on top of the consonant that it doubles. Watch Ustaaz El-Shinnawi write shadda and copy the shape he draws, then practice by copying the word حَجّ *(pilgrimage)*:

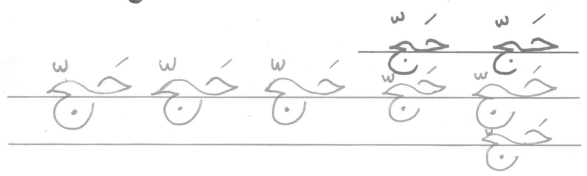

Practice writing and pronouncing shadda in these words:

(he marries) يَتَزَوَّج   (baker) خَبّاز   (I love) أُحِبّ

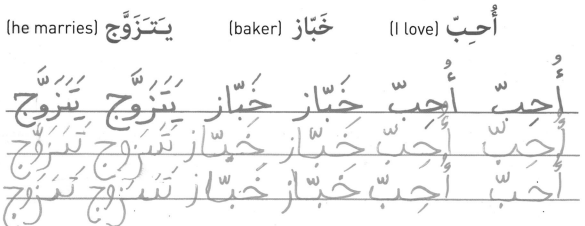

Shadda never occurs on the first consonant in a word. When it occurs in the middle of a word, it is always followed by a vowel; thus, shadda and sukuun do not occur together on the same consonant.[1] When writing the vowels on shadda, remember that fatHa and Damma are always written above the shadda. When writing shadda + kasra, you have two options: (a) the kasra may be written in its normal position beneath the line, such that the shadda sits above and the kasra below the consonant, or (b) the kasra may be written just below the shadda above the consonant.

---

[1] Formal Arabic has stricter rules about syllable and word formation than spoken Arabic, and three or more consonants in a row without a vowel are not allowed. Technically, words in formal Arabic do not end in sukuun but rather in grammatical suffixes with vowels, so, for example, the shadda at the end of the word أُحِبّ does take a vowel in formal Arabic (this is why we do not write sukuun at the end of words). In spoken Arabic, many dialects do not have a rule against consonant clusters. In other dialects, like Egyptian, a short helping vowel breaks up consonant clusters—listen for this in the colloquial scenes.

Learn to recognize both forms and choose one to use. Copy the examples:

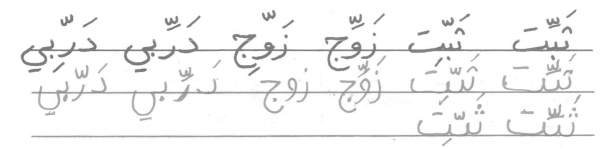

🎧 Drill 3. Dictation (At home)

Using the video, write below the words you see and hear, including all vowels. Watch and listen as many times as necessary.

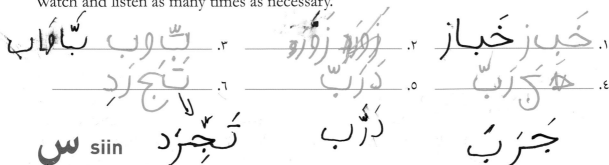

Siin (pronounced like English *seen*) is the name of the Arabic letter that corresponds to English *s*, as in the word *seen* itself. However, remember that English *s* is often pronounced as *z*, such as in *easy* and *optimism*, and in many plurals like *dogs* and *bugs*. Arabic س, on the other hand, always retains the soft *ss* sound. س is a frontal consonant, which means that surrounding vowels take a frontal quality, especially alif and fatHa, which sound like *e* in *bet*.

🎧 Listening Exercise 3. Reading س (At home)

Listen to and read aloud words containing س.

١. سـادات ٢. بَـسّ ٣. سُـبـات ٤. وَسْواس ٥. حَسَـد

🎧 Writing

سس

سـس سـس س سـس

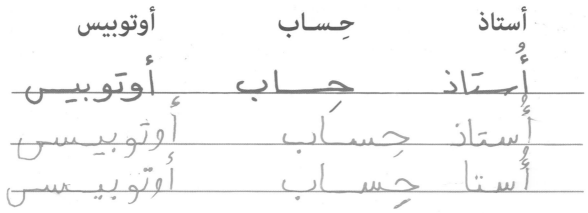

س is a connecting letter that is distinguished in print by its three "teeth." In handwriting, however, س is often written without its teeth, as a long straight line, although this varies according to regional practice or personal preference. In either case, it takes a tail when written in independent or in final position. Compare the printed and handwritten forms of the following:

أوتوبيس حِساب أستاذ

You will quickly become accustomed to reading س (with its teeth) in print. We suggest that you learn to handwrite it without the teeth so you get accustomed to reading it that way in handwriting, too. Watch Ustaaz El-Shinnawi write the forms of س and imitate what he does. To write independent س, begin on the line and draw a very small hook, just enough to indicate the beginning of a letter. Continue into the long, flat body, then dip below the line into the tail, making sure that it comes all the way back up to the line in a full semicircle. Practice writing the word دَرس *(lesson)*:

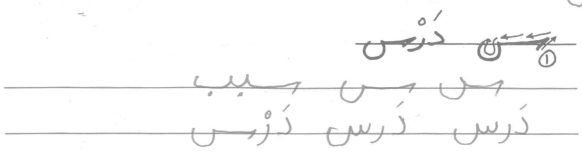

Initial س is written just like independent س but without the tail. The body of initial ـس merges into the connecting segment so that the two are indistinguishable, so make sure to lengthen the body of the letter. Practice writing initial ـس in the word أسوَد *(black)*:

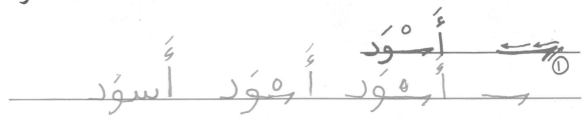

When ـس is connected from a previous letter, the connecting segment and the body of the letter are indistinguishable and **there is no hook on the beginning,** so that the connecting segment and the letter together form a flat line like this: _____. The body of this toothless ـسـ must be long enough to distinguish it from a connecting segment. **Remember: In handwriting,** a flat line _____ represents ـسـ , but in **print,** a flat line without teeth does **not** represent ـسـ . Copy this connecting handwritten form in the word حِسَاب *(arithmetic)*:

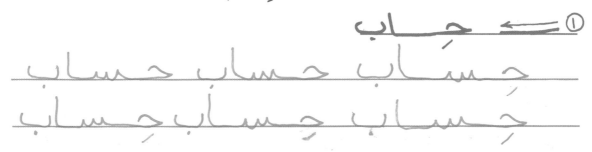

Final س is written with its tail, which **must come all the way back up to the line** (otherwise it might be mistaken for ـر). Copy final س ـس in the colloquial word بَسّ *(that's all, enough)*:

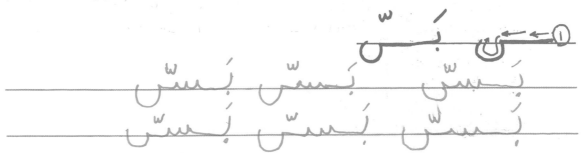

🎧 Drill 4. Dictation (At home)

Using the video, write below the words you see and hear, including all vowels and shadda. Watch and listen as many times as necessary.

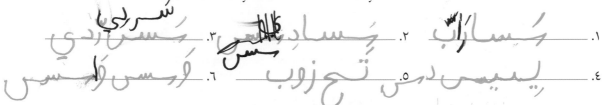

Never start a word with a س ‿‿‿

ش shiin

This letter corresponds to the sound *sh* in *shoe*.

🎧 Listening Exercise 4. Hearing and pronouncing ش (At home)

Listen to and read aloud these words containing ش.

٥. رَشّـاش   ٤. حَشيـش   ٣. باشا   ٢. بَشير   ١. شِبـر

🎧 Writing

ش   ش   ش   شـ   ـشـ

The letter ش is a connector, and its shapes match those of س, except that this letter takes three dots above. In handwriting, ش is written without its teeth (like س) and the three dots are connected in a caret, just like those of ث. Watch Ustaaz El-Shinnawi and imitate his writing. Practice initial ـش by copying شـاي *(tea)*:

Copy medial and final ـشـ ش in حَشِيش *(grass)*:

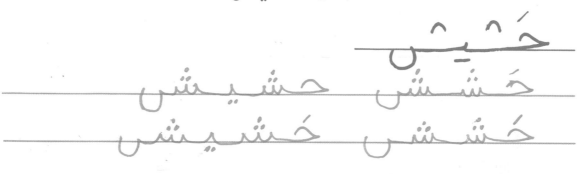

🎧 **Drill 5. Dictation (At home)**

Using the accompanying video, write below the words you see and hear, including all vowels. Watch and listen as many times as necessary.

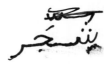

Vocabulary and Conversation: Taking Leave

New Vocabulary 1 (At home)

Listen to and learn these words:

Meaning	maSri		shaami		Formal /written	
bus		أوتوبـيـس		أوتوبـيـس		أوتوبـيـس
lesson		دَرس		دَرس		دَرس
tea		شاي		شاي		شاي
young people; "guys" (including mixed gender)		شَباب		شَباب		شَباب
good, kind-hearted (as adjective); OK, well... (as an interjection)	Tayyib	طَيِّب	Tayyib	طَيِّب	Tayyib	طَيِّب
	Tayyiba	طَيِّبة	Tayybe	طَيِّبة	Tayyiba	طَيِّبة
may I be excused? (what to say when you have to leave) (masc. / fem.)	ⁿan iznak	عن إذنَك	ⁿan iznak	عن إذنَك	ⁿan idhnika	عن إذنكَ
	ⁿan iznik	عن إذنِك	ⁿan iznik	عن إذنِك	ⁿan idhniki	عن إذنكِ
class; classroom	faSl	فَصل	Saff	صَفّ	faSl	فَصل
					Saff	صَفّ
good-bye		مَعَ السَّلامة		مَعَ السَّلامة		مَعَ السَّلامة
	maⁿa s-salaama		maⁿa s-salaame		maⁿa s-salaama	
(reply to) maⁿa s-salaama (masc./fem.)		الله يسَلّمك		الله يسَلّمك		
	allah yisallim-ak/ –ik		alla ysallm-ak/ -ik			

🎧 **Drill 6. Scene 5A:** *tayyib itfaDDali/tfaDDali*
(At-home preparation; in-class activation)

Before listening: In this scene you will see people meeting each other. What words do you expect to hear?

1. First listen: Listen to and recognize familiar words and expressions. What do you recognize? Write down what you hear.

2. Second listen: Before you listen again, think about particular parts or expressions to focus on. What do you want to check? Write down additional expressions you hear.

3. Third listen: Focus on phrases more than on single words. Do you have any more questions about how things are being said? Think about them, then listen again and write down anything new.

4. In class: After you have discussed the scene with your classmates, listen with the purpose of preparing to use the expressions you heard yourself. Focus on how things are said and repeat them aloud to rehearse.

Culture: Good-bye!

Like saying hello, taking leave or saying good-bye has a set of patterned expressions. Polite behavior requires you to excuse yourself before leaving the company of someone by saying ^c*an iznak* or ^c*an iznik*, as you saw in scene 5A. The other person then says *itfaDDal/i*, followed by *ma^ca s-salaama*. The person leaving waits for the other person to say *ma^ca s-salaama*, and replies *allaah yisallimak/ik*.

>> Letters and Sounds: Part Two

ص Saad

This letter represents the emphatic counterpart of س. Pronounce س aloud, and note the position of your tongue: It should be toward the front of and close to the roof of the mouth. Now, starting at the back of your teeth, move your tongue back along the roof of your mouth. You will find a bony ridge just behind the teeth, before the upward curve of the roof of your mouth. Put your tongue against this ridge. The rest of your tongue will drop lower inside your mouth. The emphatic or velarized consonants in Arabic are pronounced by placing the end of your tongue in this spot and dropping the rest of the tongue as low as you can.

Remember: ص and other emphatic consonants deepen the sound of surrounding vowels, most noticeably alif and fatHa, which sound like *u* in *but*. Pay attention to the sound of all vowels near this emphatic letter, because **the quality of the vowels gives the clearest indication of emphatic consonants.**

🎧 Listening Exercise 5. Hearing and pronouncing ص (At home)

Listen to and pronounce words with ص, paying particular attention to the surrounding vowels. Compare the fatHa in these words to the vowel in English *but*.

٥. حِصّة   ٤. صُوَر   ٣. صَباح   ٢. صار   ١. صـاد

🎧 Listening Exercise 6. Hearing the difference between ص and س (At home)

Listen to the contrast between س and ص in the alphabet videos several times.

🎧 Listening Exercise 7. Contrasting between س and ص (At home)

Listen to and repeat the following pairs of words contrasting س and ص. Notice that the emphatic quality of ص deepens the sound of surrounding vowels. Listening to vowel quality is the easiest way to distinguish between س and ص.

٣. يَسير / يَصير   ٢. ساح / صاح   ١. أَسبَح / أَصبَح

٥. حَسَد / حَصَد   ٤. يَسُدّ / يَصُدّ

🎧 **Drill 7. Distinguishing between** س **and** ص **(At home)**

Listen to the twelve words on the audio, each containing either س or ص . Select the letter that represents the sound you hear.

1. ص (س)   2. (ص) س   3. (ص) س   4. ص (س)

5. (ص) س   6. ص (س)   7. ص (س)   8. (ص) س

9. (ص) س   10. (ص) س   11. ص (س)   12. (ص) س

🎧 **Writing**

The letter ص is a connector, and it retains the same basic shape in both print and handwriting. There are two essential points to keep in mind when writing ص : (a) the loop must be large and oval-shaped, and (b) there should be a small "tooth" after the loop. Watch Ustaaz El-Shinnawi and imitate his hand movements.

To write independent ص , start on the line and make a big loop up and back to your right, then swing down and close it. Without stopping, make the tooth and then drop well below the line to make the tail. The tail of ص is the same shape as that of س and **must come all the way back up to the line**. Practice this new shape:

Ind.   Ini   M

Initial ـصـ is written the same way but without the tail. After making the tooth, continue to the connecting segment. Copy صَحِيح *(correct)*, and remember to start above the line so that you can continue into the حـ:

To write ‑ص connected from a previous letter, draw the connecting segment to the starting point of the loop, the same point at which you started in initial position, then follow the same steps as above. Copy, following the arrows:

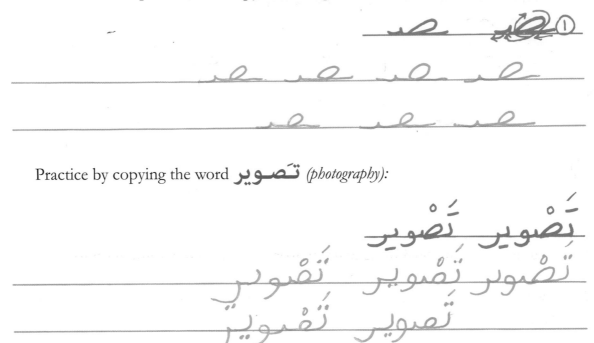

Practice by copying the word تَصْوير *(photography)*:

Final ‑ص‑ is connected the same way as medial ‑ص‑ and ends with a final tail the same shape as the tail of س.

Practice by copying شَخْص *(person)*:

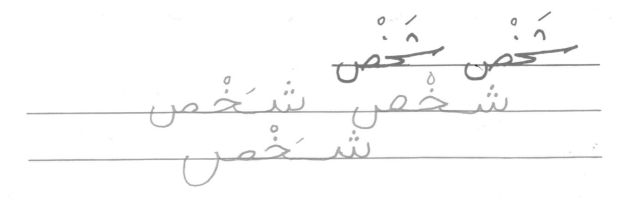

🎧 Drill 8. Identifying ص and س (At home)

Listen to the audio to hear words containing either ص or س. Choose the correct letter to complete the word. Remember to listen for vowel quality to help you distinguish between the letters.

١. ســـابِيح   ٢. بَصِـيـر   ٣. بَس   ٤. تَصـدُر

٥. يَدرُســـا   ٦. صـوْتي   ٧. أَسـبَحَ ✗   ٨. حَصــد

🎧 Drill 9. Reading س and ص (At-home preparation; in-class activation)

There are two parts to this exercise:

A. At home, listen and read these pairs of words aloud, and pay attention to س and ص.

B. In class, take turns with a partner reading a random word and ask your partner to identify it.

1. (a) سارَ   (b) صارَ   4. (a) صَبْر   (b) سَبْر

2. (a) باس   (b) باص   5. (a) خَسّ   (b) خَصّ

3. (a) أسِير   (b) أصِير   6. (a) سَدَّت   (b) صَدَّت

🎧 Drill 10. Dictation (At home)

Watch and listen to the video and write below the words you hear, including all vowels. Watch and listen as many times as necessary.

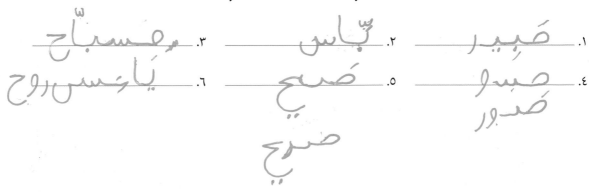

ض Daad

In the same way that ص represents the emphatic counterpart of س , the letter ض represents the emphatic counterpart of د . To pronounce ض, place your tongue in the same position as you did to say ص and say د; the result will be ض. Remember that ض is an emphatic consonant that deepens the quality of surrounding vowels, especially alif and fatHa, which will sound like *u* in *but*.

🎧 Listening Exercise 8. Hearing and pronouncing ض (At home)

Listen to and repeat aloud these words containing ض.

٥. رِياض   ٤. حَضَـر   ٣. خَضَّ   ٢. ضَباب   ١. ضـاد

🎧 Listening Exercise 9. Hearing the difference between د and ض (At home)

Listen several times to the contrast between د and ض in the alphabet videos.

🎧 Listening Exercise 10. Contrasting د and ض (At home)

Listen to and repeat the pairs of words contrasting د and ض.

٣. خَدّ / خَضّ   ٢. رِيادة / رِياضة   ١. دال / ضال

٥. دَرْب / ضَـرْب   ٤. دَبّ / ضَبّ

🎧 Drill 11. Contrasting د and ض (At home)

Listen to the twelve words on the audio, each containing either د or ض. Select the letter that represents the sound you hear.

ض د	٤.	ض د	٣.	ض د	٢.	د ض	١.
ض د	٨.	ض د	٧.	ض د	٦.	د ض	٥.
ض د	١٢.	ض د	١١.	ض د	١٠.	د ض	٩.

106

🎧 Writing

ض ض ض ض ض

ض is a connector and is written just like ص except that it takes one dot above. Watch Ustaaz El-Shinnawi and follow the same steps you did for writing ص. Practice writing the independent form:

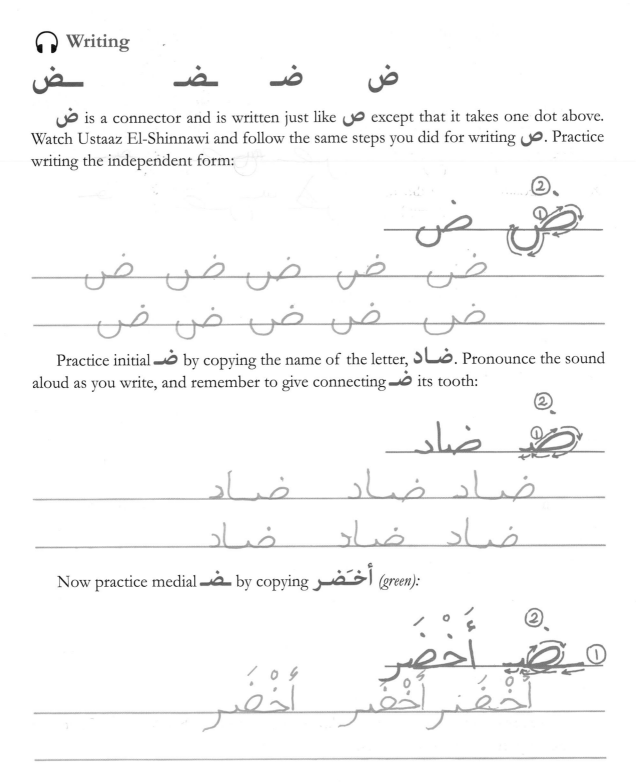

Practice initial ضـ by copying the name of the letter, ضاد. Pronounce the sound aloud as you write, and remember to give connecting ـضـ its tooth:

Now practice medial ـضـ by copying أَخَضَر (green):

Practice final ض ـض in أَبيَض (white):

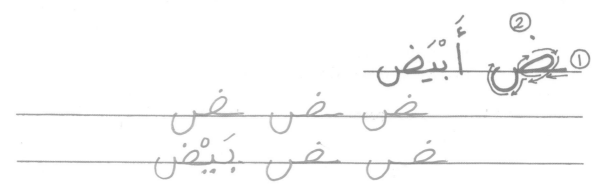

🎧 **Drill 12. Recognizing د and ض (At home)**

Listen to the words on the audio containing either د or ض. Select the correct letter to complete each word.

١. ..... باب   ٢. تَحْري.....   ٣. تُبيـ.....

٤. أَ.....رِب   ٥. ....حْر   ٦. سر.....ي

٧. تَ.....ريس   ٨. أَ.......رار   ٩. تَ.....اريس

🎧 **Drill 13. Reading aloud (At-home preparation; in-class activation)**

There are two parts to this exercise:

A. At home, listen and read these pairs of words aloud, paying attention to **د** and **ض**.

B. In class, take turns with a partner reading a random word and ask your partner to identify it.

1.	(a) رَدَّ	(b) رَضَّ
2.	(a) يَدُرُّ	(b) يَضُرُّ
3.	(a) تَحَدَّرَت	(b) تَحَضَّرَت
4.	(a) بيد	(b) بيض
5.	(a) دَرْبي	(b) ضَرْبي
6.	(a) دَجَرَ	(b) ضَجَرَ
7.	(a) حَرَّدَت	(b) حَرَّضَت
8.	(a) دَرَّس	(b) ضَرَّس

🎧 **Drill 14. Letter connection (At home)**

Connect the letters to form words. Then listen to the words and write in the short vowels you hear.

١. ص + ب + و + ر = _____ صن صبور _____

٢. ش + ب + ا + ب + ي = _____ سبابي _____

٣. أ + س + ر + ا + ر = _____ أسرار _____

٤. ت + ص + د + ي + ر = _____

٥. ا + س + ت + ي + ر + ا + د = _____

٦. خ + ي + ا + ر + و + ص = ــــــــــــــــــــ

٧. ت + ا + و + ر + ض + خ = ــــــــــــــــــــ

٨. ب + ا + ر + و + ش = ــــــــــــــــــــ

٩. ت + ا + ر + ا + ش + ا = ــــــــــــــــــــ

١٠. ح + ا + ب + ص = ــــــــــــــــــــ

١١. ي + ر + و + ص = ــــــــــــــــــــ

١٢. ر + ي + ص + ا + ر + ص = ــــــــــــــــــــ

١٣. ت + ر + ض + ر + ت = ــــــــــــــــــــ

١٤. ت + ا + ص + ص + خ + ت = ــــــــــــــــــــ

🎧 Drill 15. Dictation (At home)

Using the video, write below the words you see and hear, including all vowels. Watch and listen as many times as necessary.

٢. ــــــــــــــــــ	١. ــــــــــــــــــ
٤. ــــــــــــــــــ	٣. ــــــــــــــــــ
٦. ــــــــــــــــــ	٥. ــــــــــــــــــ
٨. ــــــــــــــــــ	٧. ــــــــــــــــــ
١٠. ــــــــــــــــــ	٩. ــــــــــــــــــ

🎧 **Drill 16. Reading aloud (At-home preparation; in-class activation)**

Read each of the following words aloud. Then, check your pronunciation by listening to the audio.

٢٥. صَحيح	١٧. صاحِب	٩. شَجَر	١. أخْـضَـر
٢٦. حِسـاب	١٨. حَواجِـز	١٠. شِـتاء	٢. خَـضْراء
٢٧. حُجّاج	١٩. ضَحايا	١١. صُراخ	٣. أبْـيَـض
٢٨. زِيارات	٢٠. ذُباب	١٢. تَشْـريح	٤. رَصاص
٢٩. صَحَّح	٢١. أصْحاب	١٣. سَبْت	٥. أسـود
٣٠. تَخَرَّج	٢٢. دُروس	١٤. صَباح	٦. تَـشَـرَبي
٣١. شاي	٢٣. ضَوْء	١٥. صَوْت	٧. شَـراب
٣٢. إخْـراج	٢٤. يُدَرِّس	١٦. صَواب	٨. بَيَّـض

Vocabulary and Conversation: Being Polite

🎧 New Vocabulary 2 (At home)

Listen to and learn these words. Notice that the masculine and feminine forms of adjectives are listed together, with masculine listed first and a slash separating the two genders. From now on, all adjectives will be listed in this manner:

Meaning	maSri	shaami	Formal /written
right! correct!	صَحّ	صَحّ	صَحيح
white	أَبْيَض	أَبْيَض	أَبْيَض
black	إسْوِد	أَسْوَد	أَسْوَد
green	أَخْضَر	أَخْضَر	أَخْضَر
thank you	شُكراً shukran	شُكراً shukran	شُكراً shukran
you're welcome	العَفو il-ᶜafw	أهلا وسهلا فيك ahla w sahla fiik/-ki	عَفواً ᶜafwan
please	مِن فَضلَك min faDlak/-ik	مِن فَضلَك min faDlak/-ik	مِن فَضلِك min faDlika/-ki
sorry!	آسِف / ة aasif / asfa	مِتْأَسِّف mit'assif مِتْأَسِّفة mit'assfe	آسِف aasif آسِفة aasifa
there is	fii فيه	fii فيه	هُناك hunaak
there isn't	ma fiish ما فيش	maa fii ما فيه	لَيسَ هُناك laysa hunaak
that's all, only	بَسّ	بَسّ	فَقَط faqaT
something	حاجة Haaga	شي	شَيء
something else	حاجة تاني Haaga taani	شي تاني shi taani	شَيء آخَر shay' aakhar

🎧 Saying "I want" in Arabic (At home)

The Arabic expressions used to say *want* vary from region to region, but all are related to formal Arabic. In many dialects, *want* is a verb. In Levantine, *want* is a noun-possessive construction (*my desire is . . .*), and in Egyptian it is an adjective (*I am wanting*).

Meaning	maSri	shaami	Formal /written
I want (masc./fem.)	أنا عايز/ة ana ᶜaayiz/ᶜayza	بِدّي	أُريد
you want (masc.)	انتَ عايِز inta ᶜaayiz	بِدَّك biddak	تُريد
you want (fem.)	انتِ عايزة inti ᶜayza	بِدِّك biddik	تُريدين turiidiin
he wants	هو عايِز huwwa ᶜaayiz	بِدُّه biddo	يُريد
she wants	هي عايزة hiyya ᶜayza	بِدّها bidda	تُريد

🎧 Drill 17. Vocabulary matching (At home)

This exercise is shown on the companion website only. Match the phrases with the pictures you see on your screen.

🎧 Drill 18. Listen and interact (At home)

Someone needs some information from you and will initiate a conversation. Use as much Arabic as you can to respond to the person's questions.

🎧 Drill 19. Scene 5B: *min faDlak* (At-home preparation;
in-class activation)

Watch scene 5B.
1. First listen: Where is this taking place? What does the second person want?
2. Second listen: What new details do you hear this time?
3. Third listen: Is the person successful in getting what she wants? Why or why not?
4. In class, listen once more with a partner and prepare to use the expressions you heard yourself. Act out a similar scene together.

🎧 Drill 20. Scene 5C: Uses of اتفضَّل (At-home preparation;
in-class activation)

Watch scene 5C, which contains various uses of the expression *itfaDDal*.
What does this expression mean in the situations you see?

Drill 21. Skits (At-home preparation; in-class presentation)

With a partner, create a skit to perform in class using as many expressions and as much vocabulary as you can. Do not use words from outside class that your classmates don't know.

>> Roots

    Arabic, like other Semitic languages, is based in part on a system of roots, which are sets of consonants that carry meaning. A root normally consists of three consonants that must occur in the same order in all the words derived from it. Every Arabic noun and verb has a root, and you should begin to pay attention to the consonants of words you learn. These roots are used in patterns that you will eventually come to recognize: noun patterns, verb patterns, and adjective patterns. As you learn more vocabulary, we will begin to introduce aspects of this "root and pattern" system. For now, focus on picking out roots of nouns, verbs, and adjectives you know. Using the words in drill 16, see if you and a partner can find the Arabic roots for the following, and two words derived from each:

1. studying/teaching: _____

2. correctness: _____

3. drinking: _____

4. whiteness: _____

5. greenness: _____

الوحدة السادسة
Unit Six

In this unit:

Gender and taa marbuuTa ة

Letters ط ظ ع غ

Vocabulary and Conversation: Coffee Time

Culture: At the Coffeehouse

Describing with Adjectives

Letters and Sounds: Part One

Gender in Arabic

You have learned that all nouns are either masculine or feminine, and that nouns that describe humans have both masculine or feminine forms to reflect the person's natural gender. You also know that adjectives have masculine and feminine forms to allow them to agree with the nouns they modify. Adjectives must always agree in gender with their nouns. Fortunately, gender is easy to predict in Arabic, because almost all feminine nouns and adjectives end in the feminine marker taa marbuuTa.

ة taa marbuuTa

This symbol is not considered to be a part of the Arabic alphabet because its function is primarily grammatical. It can only occur at the end of nouns and adjectives. This letter is called taa marbuuTa, meaning *the tied* ت, and it almost always indicates feminine gender.[1] As its name and form indicate, it is related to the letter ت, and sometimes it is pronounced as ت (in possessive constructions, which you will learn soon). At other times it is not pronounced as ت, **but the fatHa vowel that always precedes ة is always pronounced**. In spoken Arabic, a fatHa at the end of a word will almost always indicate ة. **Remember**: When you hear a noun that ends with a fatHa sound, you can usually assume that it is feminine and spelled with a ة.

🎧 **Listening Exercise 1. Reading words with ة (At home)**

Listen to and read aloud words ending in ة.[2]

صورة .٥   شَجَرة .٤   زَوجة .٣   وَردة .٢   أُستاذة .١

🎧 **Drill 1. Listening for ة (At home)**

Listen to the audio to hear nine words. For each, select Yes if you hear ة and No if you do not.

1. (Yes) No   2. Yes (No)   3. (Yes) No   4. Yes (No)   5. (Yes) No

6. (Yes) No   7. Yes (No)   8. (Yes) (No)   9. (Yes) No

---

[1]The taa marbuuTa has another function in classical Arabic, and that is to mark intensity or exceptionality. The few masculine words that end in taa marbuuTa are survivors from classical Arabic.

[2]In Levantine dialects, this fatHa vowel is pronounced *e* (between fatHa and kasra), except after emphatic consonants.

🎧 Writing

ة ـة

Since ة only occurs in word-final position, it has only two shapes: one that follows connecting letters and one that follows nonconnectors. Watch Ustaaz El-Shinnawi write ة. As you can see, the two dots that appear separately in print are usually drawn together as a short horizontal bar in handwriting (just like the dots of ت and ي). To write ة after a nonconnecting letter, start at the top of the letter and draw the loop down to your right and back up. Practice by imitating Ustaaz El-Shinnawi, then copy the independent form and the word أستـاذة :

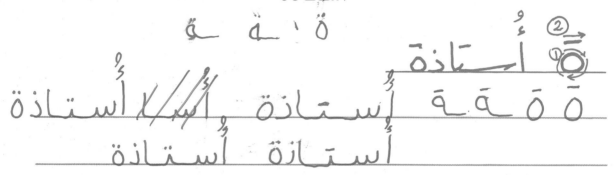

To write ة connected to a previous letter, start at the connecting segment, draw the right side of the loop up into a point, then swing back down to your left to close the loop. The shape of this loop is usually lopsided and not as round as when ة is written alone, and individual handwriting styles vary. Copy and practice the word حبيبة as shown:

Now copy and read aloud the following feminine nouns and adjectives ending in ة:

جارة   جَديدة   دجاجة   صحيحة   سَيِّدة

سَيِّدة صَحيحة دَجاجة جَديدة جارة

سَيِّدة صحيحة دَجاجة/جَديدة/جارة

سَيِّدة صحيحة دَجاجة جَديدة جارة

ط Taa

This letter represents the emphatic counterpart of ت. To pronounce it, put the tip of your tongue up against the bony ridge behind your teeth on the roof of your mouth, the same position used for ض, and drop your tongue low in your mouth. Try to say *t* holding this position. The result will be ط. The difference in pronunciation between ط and ت parallels that between ض and د. **Remember**: ط is an emphatic sound that deepens the quality of surrounding vowels.

🎧 Listening Exercise 2. Contrasting ت and ط (At home)

Listen to the alphabet videos several times to hear the contrast between ت and ط.

🎧 Listening Exercise 3. Pronouncing ط (At home)

Listen to and repeat out loud words containing ط.

١. طَبيب   ٢. طالِب   ٣. رُطوبة   ٤. بَطّيخ   ٥. ضابِط   ٦. شُباط

Remember: Since ط is an emphatic letter, it affects the quality of surrounding vowels, so that fatHa in words containing ط sound like *u* in *but* and contrasts with fatHa in words with ت , which sound like *e* in *bet*.

🎧 **Listening Exercise 4. Contrasting ت and ط (At home)**

Listen to the pairs of words contrasting ت and ط.

٣. رَتَّب / رَطَّب   ٢. شَتّ / شَطّ   ١. تاب / طاب

٥. حَتّ / حَطّ   ٤. سَتْر / سَطْر

🎧 **Drill 2. Recognizing ط (At home)**

Listen to the pairs of words and select the letter of the word that contains ط.

1. a b   2. a b   3. a b   4. a b   5. a b
6. a b   7. a b   8. a b   9. a b   10. a b

🎧 **Drill 3. Identifying ط (At home)**

Listen to the ten words on the audio. For each, select Yes if you hear ط and No if you do not.

1. Yes   No   2. Yes   No   3. Yes   No   4. Yes   No
5. Yes   No   6. Yes   No   7. Yes   No   8. Yes   No
9. Yes   No   10. Yes   No

🎧 **Writing**

ط   ط   ط   ط

ط is a connector and is written in two separate steps. It is important for you to follow these steps, otherwise you will not be able to connect this letter properly. Follow Ustaaz El-Shinnawi and imitate the way he writes ط . The loop that forms the body is written in one motion, connected to the rest of the word, and the vertical line is written afterwards, much like crossing the *t* in cursive English. Do **not** write ط by beginning at the top with the downstroke, because this shape does **not** look Arabic.

To write independent ط start on the line and make the loop first. It should be large, oval, and should rest along the line lengthwise, as you see. The final step in writing ط is the downstroke. After forming the loop, **lift up your pen** and draw this stroke as you draw the alif, from the top down. Aim the downstroke at or near the left end of the loop. Write independent ط following the example:

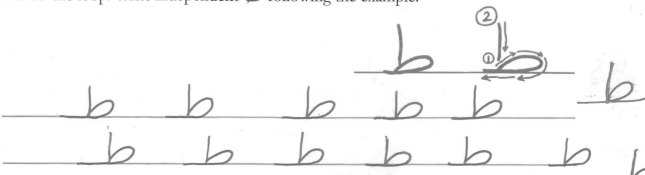

To write a word beginning with ط, begin exactly as you did above and continue into a smooth, connecting segment **without stopping to write the downstroke.** Unlike ص and ض, this letter **does not have a tooth** between the loop and the connecting segment. Write طَيِّب as the example shows:

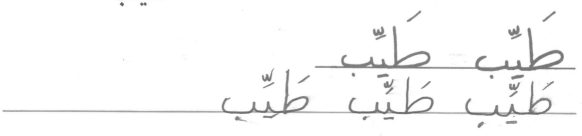

When writing ط in medial position, start from the connecting segment, continue along the line, and **without lifting the pen**, loop backwards and around to the line again to continue on to the next letter. Do not stop to write the downstroke until you have finished writing the body of the word. Like dotting the *i* or crossing the *t* in English script, this is done at the end, as the example shows. Copy the word سَطْر *(line)*:

In final position, ط ends just past the oval in a rather stubby tail. Copy final ط in the word بَطّ (*duck*):

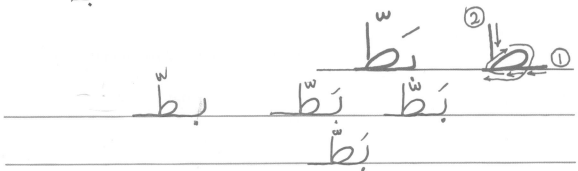

Now copy the following words containing ط in initial, medial, and final positions, following the steps you practiced. Examples:

خَطّ (handwriting)   يَطير (he flies)   طَبيب (doctor)

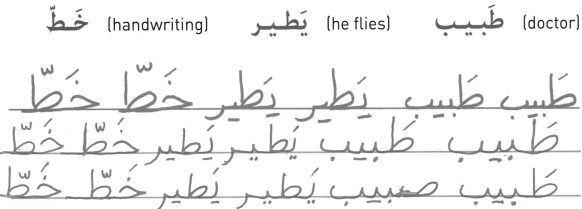

🎧 **Drill 4. Identifying** ت **and** ط **(At home)**

Listen to the audio to hear words containing either ت or ط and select the correct letter to complete the word.

١. حَ......ب   ٢. راب......ة   ٣. ...... زْخَر

٤. خَ......   ٥. ......بْشورة   ٦. سُ......ور

٧. دُسْ......ور   ٨. شِ......اء   ٩. بُحَ......

🎧 **Drill 5. Reading words with** ت **and** ط **(At-home preparation; in-class activation)**

There are two parts to this exercise:

A. At home, listen and read these pairs of words aloud, and pay attention to ت and ط.

B. In class, take turns with a partner with one of you reading a random word and the other identifying it.

1. (a) أَوْتَار   (b) أَوْطَار
2. (a) رَتِيب   (b) رَطِيب
3. (a) وَتْوَات   (b) وَطْوَاط
4. (a) بَتّ   (b) بَطّ
5. (a) وَتَّرَ   (b) وَطَّدَ
6. (a) أَتْرَحَ   (b) أَطْرَحَ
7. (a) تَيَّار   (b) طَيَّار
8. (a) تـوب   (b) طـوب

🎧 **Drill 6. Dictation (At home)**

Watch the video and write below the words you see and hear, including all vowels. Watch and listen as many times as necessary.

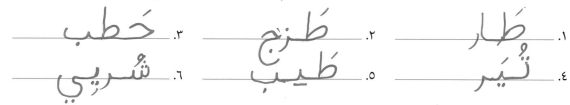

ظ DHaa

This letter represents the emphatic counterpart of ذ. Place your tongue in the same position as you did for ط, and say ذ. The tip of your tongue should be between your teeth, but the rest of your tongue should remain in the same position as for ط, low in the mouth. **Remember:** ظ is an emphatic sound that deepens the quality of the surrounding vowels.[3]

🎧 Listening Exercise 5. Pronouncing ظ (At home)

Listen to ظ in these words and repeat, and give special attention to vowel quality.

١. أَبو ظَبي   ٢. ظالِم   ٣. شَظِيّة   ٤. حَظّ   ٥. ظُهور

🎧 Listening Exercise 6. Contrasting ذ and ظ (At home)

Listen to the contrast between ذ and ظ several times.

🎧 Listening Exercise 7. Contrasting words with ذ and ظ (At home)

Listen to the contrast between ذ and ظ in the pairs of words and repeat.

١. ذال / ظاء   ٢. ذَنَب / ظَنّ   ٣. حَذَر / حَظَر

٤. ذَلّ / ظَلّ   ٥. نَذَر / نَظَر

🎧 Drill 7. Recognizing ظ (At home)

Listen to the pairs of words and select the letter of the word that contains ظ.

1. a b   2. a b   3. a b   4. a b
5. a b   6. a b   7. a b   8. a b
9. a b   10. a b

---

[3]In some urban dialects of spoken Arabic, this sound is pronounced as emphatic Z, which we will indicate with an uppercase Z. You will hear this sound in the New Vocabulary in the word maZbuuT.

🎧 Writing

Like ﻃ , the letter ﻇ is a connector and is written like ﻃ in all positions, with the addition of one dot above the body. Watch Ustaaz El-Shinnawi and imitate his movements. Independent and final ﻇ have the same truncated "tail" as ﻃ. Follow the arrows to write independent ﻇ:

When writing connected ﻇ, **do not stop** to "cross" and dot ﻇ until you have finished writing the skeleton of the word. Copy the name of the Arab Emirate, أَبــو ظَبــي , as shown:

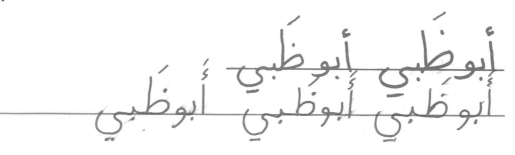

Copy and sound out the Levantine word بوظة *(ice cream)*:

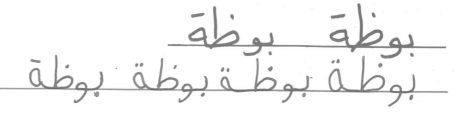

Final ظ has the same truncated "tail" that ط has. Copy final ظ in the word حَظّ *(luck)*, and finish writing the entire consonant skeleton before you go back and draw the downstroke, then dot:

🎧 Listening Exercise 8. Recognition of ث , ذ , ض , and ظ (At home)

Listen to these words to review these sounds:

1.   (a) ظَبْي   (b) ضَابِط   (c) ذابَت   (d) ثابِت
2.   (a) حَظَر   (b) حَضَر   (c) حَذَر   (d) حَثَّ
3.   (a) بَظّ   (b) بَضّ   (c) بَذّ   (d) بَثّ

🎧 Drill 8. Distinguishing ث , ذ , ض , and ظ (At home)

Listen to the audio to hear ten words. For each, select the letter that represents the sound you hear.

1.   ظ   ض   ذ   ث   2.   ظ   ض   ذ   ث
3.   ظ   ض   ذ   ث   4.   ظ   ض   ذ   ث
5.   ظ   ض   ذ   ث   6.   ظ   ض   ذ   ث
7.   ظ   ض   ذ   ث   8.   ظ   ض   ذ   ث
9.   ظ   ض   ذ   ث   10.   ظ   ض   ذ   ث

🎧 **Drill 9. Reading ث , ذ , and ظ (At-home preparation; in-class activation)**

Listen to the audio and read the words aloud, paying attention to ث , ذ , and ظ:

1. (a) ثَبَتَ (b) ذُباب (c) ظَبْية
2. (a) حُثّي (b) حوذي (c) حَظّي
3. (a) يَحُثّ (b) يَحذو (c) يَحظو
4. (a) أَثَّرَ (b) حَذَّرَ (c) حَظَّرَ

🎧 **Drill 10. Identifying ث , ذ , and ظ (At home)**

Listen to the audio to hear words containing ث , ذ , or ظ. Choose the correct letter to complete the word you hear.

٢. تَحْ......ـير

٤. أ......ـواب

٦. ......بْت

٨. إِ......بات

١٠. حِ......اء

١. ......

٣. ......

٥. ......ـرِياء

٧. بُ......ـور

٩. جَ......ـوة

🎧 **Drill 11. Dictation (At home)**

Watch the video and write below the words you hear, including all vowels. Watch and listen as many times as necessary.

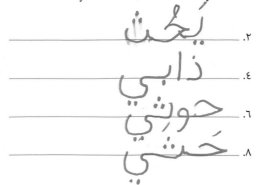

٢. يَعُـثّ

٤. ذابي

٦. حوذي

٨. حَثّي

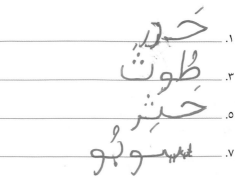

١. حَـذِر

٣. طُـوث

٥. حَـثِـر

٧. ......

Drill 12. Reading aloud (In class)

Before reading aloud the following pairs of nouns, look at both of them at the same time and see if you can identify the root (some of them will have roots with و or ي , and not all the roots will be identifiable right now. Skip the ones that are difficult). After you have finished, read each pair aloud. What is the relationship between the two words?

١. ضَرورة / ضَرورات   ٧. شَيْخ / شُيوخ   ١٣. طَبيبة / طَبيبات

٢. دار / دور   ٨. جُثّة / جُثَث   ١٤. سَيّارة / سَيّارات

٣. حِزْب / أحْزاب   ٩. واجِب / واجِبات   ١٥. طَيْر / طُيور

٤. طَبيب / أطِبّاء   ١٠. حاجّ / حُجّاج   ١٦. يَخْت / يُخوت

٥. صورة / صُوَر   ١١. أُسْتاذة / أُستاذات   ١٧. ضابِط / ضُبّاط

٦. أُسْتاذ / أَساتِذة   ١٢. حارة / حارات   ١٨. ظَبْية / ظِباء

Vocabulary and Conversation: Coffee Time

New Vocabulary 1

Listen to and learn these words. Notice that the qaaf in qahwa is pronounced as a hamza in both Cairo and Damascus; this pronunciation of qaaf is widespread in the urban dialects of Egypt and the Levant.

Meaning	maSri		shaami		Formal /written	
ready	gaahiz/gahza	جاهِز/ة	jaahiz/jaahze	جاهِز/ة	jaahiz/a	جاهِز/ة
coffee	'ahwa	قَهوة	'ahwe	قَهوة	qahwa	قَهْوة
milk	laban	لَبن	Haliib	حَليب	Haliib	حَليب
sugar	sukkar	سُكَّر	sikkar	سِكَّر	sukkar	سُكَّر
medium sugar	maZbuuT	مَضبوط	sikkar wasaT	سِكَّر وَسَط	sukkar wasaT	سُكَّر وَسَط
juice	ᶜaSiir	عَصير	ᶜaSiir	عَصير	ᶜaSiir	عَصير
water	mayya	مَيّة	mayy	مَيّ	maa'	ماء
Let's go!	yalla; yalla biina	يَللا ؛ يللا بينا	yalla	يَللا	hayyaa binaa	هَيّا بِنا
I go		آروح		آروح	adhhab	أذهَب
you (masc.) go		تِروح		تروح	tadhhab	تَذهَب
you (fem.) go		تروحي		تروحي	tadhhabiin	تَذهَبين
he goes		يِروح		يروح	yadhhab	يَذهَب
she goes		تِروح		تروح	tadhhab	تَذهَب
I drink		أشرَب		إشرَب	ashrab	أشرَب

Meaning	maSri	shaami	Formal /written
you (masc.) drink	تِشرَب	تِشرَب	تَشرَب
you (fem.) drink	تِشرَبي	تِشرَبي	تَشرَبين tashrabiin
he drinks	يِشرَب	يِشرَب	يَشرَب
she drinks	تِشرَب	تِشرَب	تَشرَب

Example sentences:

بدي اشرب قهوة   بتحب تشرب شاي؟

بدي اروح عالبيت   عايز اروح البيت   عايزة تشربي ايه؟

🎧 **Drill 13. Scene 6: yalla! (At-home preparation; in-class activation)**

After you have studied the new vocabulary, watch scene 6.

1. First listen: What is the situation?
2. Second listen: What new expressions do you hear?
3. Third listen: Plan your strategy beforehand. What sentences or phrases do you want to hear better? Write down the part of the sentence or phrase you know and listen to it again until you can write down the rest.
4. In class: After discussing the scene with your classmates, listen together once more in preparation to act out a similar scene with others.

🎧 Culture: tishrab ahwa?

Coffee and tea are the most popular social drinks in the Arab world. They are served to visitors at home and in the workplace. The choice between coffee and tea is partly a matter of local custom and supply, and partly a matter of personal taste. In much of North Africa, tea is more common and is often made very sweet with loose green tea and mint. In restaurants, coffee is usually served European style.

In Egypt and the Levant, Arabic coffee (also called Turkish coffee) is a strong drink made from very finely ground, dark beans boiled in a little pot, and often served in demitasse cups or glasses. Watch the video to see how it is made. In Egypt, unless you request otherwise, coffee will be served to you maZbuuT, which means *just right*, referring to the amount of sugar (about one teaspoon per small cup). Tea is also popular and is served sweet.

In the Arabian Peninsula, another kind of Arabic coffee is served. The coffee beans are roasted in a different manner and the coffee itself is almost clear in color and has a unique flavor. It is served in tiny cups without handles, and the cup is refilled by the host until the guest signals that he or she has had enough by tilting it from side to side several times.

Culture: At the coffeehouse

Coffeehouses are popular meeting places, although by custom they are frequented more by men than by women in most Arab countries (women tend to socialize privately in homes). However, it is now common in many urban areas to see young men and young women in upscale cafés smoking the water pipe, called *shiisha* or *argiile*, which is enjoying a new wave of popularity among young people. In addition to coffee, tea, and other hot drinks, games such as chess and backgammon are available in traditional coffeehouses. Watch the video to see scenes from some traditional coffeehouses around Cairo.

>> Letters and Sounds: Part Two

ع ʿayn

We now come to one of the most distinctive sounds in Arabic: ع. When pronounced correctly, ع has its own unique beauty and can be a very expressive sound. The degree to which ع is emphasized differs slightly from one dialect area to another; in the Gulf and in some areas of North Africa, it is pronounced with a greater constricting of the muscles and has a more powerful sound. It is not difficult to pronounce but you need to exercise the same throat muscles that you use to pronounce ح. You should still be practicing the exercises you learned above for ح, in which you constrict your throat muscles as if you were blocking off the air passage from the inside. You can feel this by putting your hand on your throat. Say ح, and feel the muscles contract. Now pronounce the same sound and voice it, that is, instead of a breathy sound, make a deep, throaty sound. Keep your hand on your throat so that you can feel your muscles contract. Also, if you bend your head down so that your chin rests on your chest, you will be able to feel and hear what you are doing more easily. Use the alphabet chart and then listen and watch the pronunciation of ع.

🎧 Listening Exercise 9. Pronouncing ع (At home)

Listen to and read aloud the words containing ع in various positions.

١. عَرَبي   ٢. عَيْب   ٣. عاد   ٤. يَعـود

٥. ســاعـة   ٦. رَعْي   ٧. دَع

It is helpful to put your hand on your throat so that you can feel the muscles contract every time you say ع for the next few weeks, until you are accustomed to the sound. ع is a very important sound in Arabic, and you must learn to say it properly in order to be understood. The more you practice now, the sooner ع will become natural for you.

🎧 Listening Exercise 10. Contrasting ء and ع (At home)

Listen to the following pairs of words and repeat, paying attention to the pronunciation of ء and ع. **Remember** that hamza is a sound you produce naturally, without effort. Say *uh-oh* before pronouncing ﺀ, and put your hand on your throat when pronouncing ع.

٣. أَسِيـر / عَسِير ٢. تَأَثَّرَ / تَعَثَّرَ ١. وَأَدَ / وَعَدَ

٥. أَطَّر / عَطَّر ٤. أَبَد / عَبَد

Drill 14. Identifying ﺀ and ع (At home)

Listen to the audio to hear nine words. For each, select the letter that matches the sound you hear.

1. ع ﺀ
2. ع ﺀ
3. ع ﺀ
4. ع ﺀ
5. ع ﺀ
6. ع ﺀ
7. ع ﺀ
8. ع ﺀ
9. ع ﺀ

Writing

ع ـﻌ ـع ع

As you can see, the letter ع is a connecting letter whose shape varies somewhat depending on its position. It is important to distinguish between the connected and unconnected shapes of ع. Watch Ustaaz El-Shinnawi as he writes the various shapes of this letter and imitate his motions.

In independent and initial positions, the common element is a c-shape that rests on the line. As an independent letter, ع takes a tail. When connected to a following letter, it leads into a connecting segment as shown. Practice writing and pronouncing independent ع in the word شَارِع *(street)*:

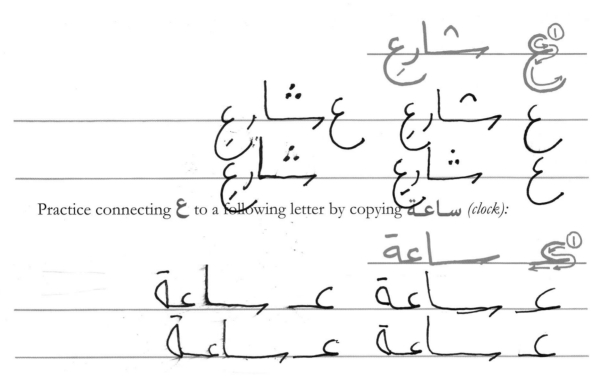

Practice connecting ع to a following letter by copying ساعة *(clock)*:

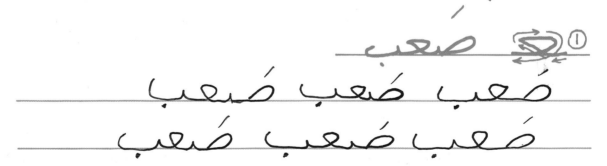

When ـعـ is connected from a previous letter in medial and final positions, the body of the letter becomes a closed loop. Rather than a c-shape, the left side of the body comes to a point, while the right side may be pointed as well or slightly curved. In some calligraphy styles the body appears filled in but most people write it open as the example shows. Practice writing the shape of medial ـعـ in the word صَعب *(difficult)*:

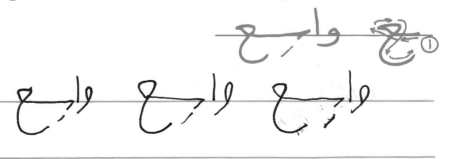

In final position, ع reassumes its tail. Practice by writing واسِع *(wide)*:

🎧 **Drill 15. Contrasting** ء **and** ع **in words**

(At-home preparation; in-class activation)

There are two parts to this exercise:

A. At home, listen and read these pairs of words aloud, and pay attention to ع and ء.

B. In class, take turns with a partner reading a random word and ask your partner to identify it.

	(a)		(b)	
1.	(a)	أَيَّدت	(b)	عَيَّدت
2.	(a)	إبْرة	(b)	عِبْرة
3.	(a)	تَأَطَّرَ	(b)	تَعَطَّرَ
4.	(a)	رَأْي	(b)	رَعْي
5.	(a)	جاءَت	(b)	جاعَت
6.	(a)	أَزيـز	(b)	عَزيـز
7.	(a)	جَأْجَأَ	(b)	جَعْجَع
8.	(a)	شاءَ	(b)	شاعَ
9.	(a)	صَدَأ	(b)	صَدَعَ
10.	(a)	أَجْزَأَت	(b)	أَجْزَعَت

🎧 **Drill 16. Distinguishing between** ء **and** ع **(At home)**

Listen to the audio to hear words containing either ء or ع and choose the correct letter to complete the word.

١. ....طُر   ٢. رَ.....د   ٣. شارِ.....

٤. .....حِبّ   ٥. .....ودي   ٦. دَ.....وات

٧. صَـ.....ب   ٨. ثَ.....ري   ٩. تَسَ.....ير

🎧 **Drill 17. Dictation** (At home)

Watch and listen to the audio and write below the words you hear, including all vowels. Watch and listen as many times as necessary.

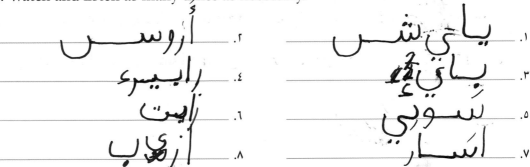

غ ghayn

This letter represents a sound similar to that of خ, and is also similar to the sound you make when you gargle. Gargle for a minute and pay attention to the muscles that you use. غ is pronounced using these same muscles in similar fashion. You may also think of this sound as a voiced خ . The difference between voiced and unvoiced consonants is a vibration of the vocal cords, and you can hear this difference in the sounds *k* in *kite* and *g* in *game*: *k* is unvoiced and *g* is voiced. Pronounce *k* and *g* several times, paying attention to how your voice changes when you say *g*. Now say خ several times, then voice it.

🎧 **Listening Exercise 11. Contrasting** غ **and** خ (At home)

Listen several times to the contrast between غ and خ in the alphabet videos.

🎧 **Listening Exercise 12. Pronouncing** غ (At home)

Listen to and read aloud the words containing غ in various positions.

٣. صَغير   ٢. بَغداد   ١. غَريب

٦. غُربة   ٥. تَبْغ   ٤. طاغي

🎧 Listening Exercise 13. Contrasting غ and خ in words (At home)

Listen to and repeat these words contrasting the sounds غ and خ:

١. يَغِيب / يَخِيب   ٢. غَضّ / خَضّ

٣. يُغَرِّب / يُخَرِّب   ٤. تَغُصّ / تَخُصّ

🎧 Writing

غ   غـ   غـ   ـغـ   ـغ

The letter غ is a connector and has the same shapes as ع, except that it takes a single dot above. Watch Ustaaz El-Shinnawi and copy independent غ as shown:

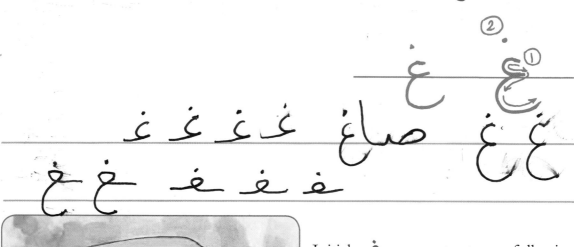

Initial غـ connects to a following letter, as Ustaaz El-Shinnawi shows. Practice writing and pronouncing the word غريب *(strange)*. Do not stop to dot until you have finished writing the entire word:

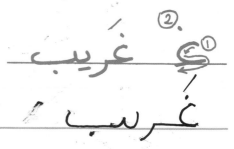

Medial غ is written just like medial ع. Watch Ustaaz El-Shinnawi, then copy and pronounce صَغير *(small, little)*:

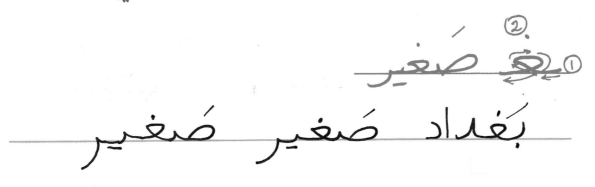

Final غ assumes the long tail, just like ع. Practice by copying and saying تَبْغ *(tobacco)*:

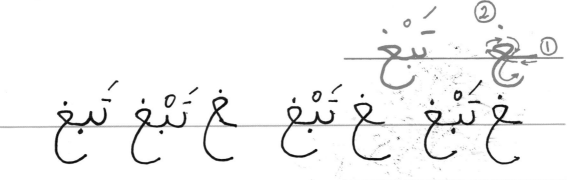

🎧 **Drill 18. Distinguishing between غ and خ (At home)**

Listen to the audio to hear nine words. For each, select the letter that corresponds to the sound you hear.

1. خ   غ   2. خ   غ   3. خ   غ
4. خ   غ   5. خ   غ   6. خ   غ
7. خ   غ   8. خ   غ   9. خ   غ

🎧 **Drill 19. Reading words with** غ **and** خ **(At-home preparation; in-class activation)**

There are two parts to this exercise:

A. At home, listen and read these pairs of words aloud, and pay attention to غ and خ.

B. In class, take turns with a partner reading a random word and ask your partner to identify it.

	(b)		(a)	
تَغريب	(b)	تَخريب	(a)	.١
يَشغُر	(b)	يَشخُر	(a)	.٢
غَيْري	(b)	خَيْري	(a)	.٣
بَغْت	(b)	بَخْت	(a)	.٤
غَيْبة	(b)	خَيْبة	(a)	.٥
رَغْوة	(b)	رَخْوة	(a)	.٦
غَرير	(b)	خَرير	(a)	.٧
تَغُطّ	(b)	تَخُطّ	(a)	.٨
غَبَّط	(b)	خَبَّط	(a)	.٩
غَضير	(b)	خَضير	(a)	.١٠

🎧 **Drill 20. Identifying** غ **and** خ **(At home)**

Listen to the audio to hear words containing either غ or خ and choose the correct letter to complete the word.

٣. ..... زّة   ٢. تَ.....يُّر   ١. صَ.....ير

٦. طا.....ـية   ٥. .....ـياطة   ٤. شـ.....ـب

٩. ضَ.....ـط   ٨. تَ.....ـرُجي   ٧. سُـ.....ـرية

Drill 21. Letter connection (At home)

Connect the letters to form words and sound them out.

١. صَ + ر + ا + ح + ة = _____

٢. تَ + غَ + يُّ + ر + ا + ت = _____

٣. بَ + ع + ي + د = _____

٤. شَ + خْ + صِ + يّ + ة = _____

٥. اِ + سْ + تَ + غْ + رَ + ب = _____

٦. طُ + ر + و + د + ي = _____

٧. غَ + رْ + بِ + يّ + ة = _____

٨. أَ + طِ + بّ + ا + ء = _____

٩. شَ + ظ + ا + ي + ا = _____

١٠. ضَ + و + ا + ح + ي = _____

١١. تَ + ضْ + غ + ي + ر = _____

١٢. تَ + خَ + صُّ + ص = _____

١٣. رُ + سْ + غ = _____

🎧 Drill 22. Word recognition (At home)

Listen to the audio to hear nine words. Select the word you hear in each row.

1.	غَرَب	خَرَب	جَرَب	حَرب
2.	ضَرَس	دَرَّس	دَرَز	دَرَس
3.	أَسبَح	اطبَع	إصبَع	أَصبَح
4.	ذاع	طاع	ضاع	شاع
5.	صَغير	سَرير	صَرير	شِرّير
6.	حُثّ	جِصّ	حِصّ	حِسّ
7.	حَذَر	حَضَر	حَظَر	حَضَر
8.	ضَبي	سَبي	صَبي	ظَبي
9.	غَبَّر	عِبَر	عَبَّر	أَبَّر

🎧 Drill 23. Dictation (At home)

Watch the video and write below the words you hear, including all vowels. Watch and listen as many times as necessary.

١. تاحمي

٢. خيايسر

٣. اعايير

٤. سسحير

٥. بجات

٦. الاب ضياك

٧. شسرع

٨. خاربي

٩. سائير

١٠. يسيياخ

Vocabulary and Conversation: Describing with Adjectives

🎧 New Vocabulary 2

Listen to and learn these words:

Meaning	maSri	shaami	Formal /written
car, automobile	عَرَبيّة	سَيّارة	سَيّارة
watch, clock; hour	ساعة	ساعة	ساعة
tree	شَجَرة	شَجَرة	شَجَرة
strange	غَريب/ة	غَريب/ة	غَريب/ة
small; young	صُغَيَّر/ة	صغير/ة	صَغير/ة
large; old (of people)	كِبير/ة kibiir/a	كبير/ة kbiir/e	كَبير/ة kabiir/a
easy	سَهْل/ة sahl/a	سَهل/ة sahl/e	سَهْل/ة sahl/a
difficult; hard	صَعب/ة	صَعب/ة	صَعْب/ة
wide; spacious	واسِع/ة	واسِع/ة	واسِع/ة

🎧 Drill 24. Vocabulary matching (At home)

This exercise is on the companion website only. Listen to the phrases and match them with most appropriate picture.

Drill 25. Describing with adjectives (At home)

By now you know that the adjectives agree in gender with the nouns they describe. Practice using adjectives in this way by writing a list of 10 things you *have* or that you *want* from among the words you know (car, house, teacher, and so on). Be specific by using at least one adjective with each noun, and remember to match the gender of your nouns and adjectives. Gender agreement takes a lot of practice, and you will have to think about it whenever you are speaking or writing. Remember that the feminine noun-adjective pairs will "rhyme" with ة .

Drill 26. Vocabulary practice (At-home preparation; in-class activation)

Prepare to ask your classmates questions using the new vocabulary, and be prepared to give your answer too. Your questions might include:

Where do they want to go?

Where do they like to drink coffee?

How do they like to drink coffee? Tea?

Do they have a car? Is it new/big/spacious?

After you have interviewed several classmates, report back to the class.

🎧 Drill 27. Listen and interact (At home)

Scenario: You are in a café in Egypt or Syria, and a waiter will come to take your order. Respond to the waiter's questions using as much Arabic as you can.

Drill 28. Reading aloud (In class)

Read the following phrases that all contain words that you now know. Read silently, first for comprehension, then aloud for pronunciation. Try to look at and identify each word as a whole rather than letter by letter or syllable by syllable.

When you read aloud, read the entire phrase without pausing between words.

١. أستاذة طيّبة   ٢. جار غريب!

٣. باب أخضر   ٤. دجاج طيّب!

٥. سيارة واسعة   ٦. تشرب شاي؟

٧. درس صعب   ٨. أخبار حبيبي

٩. صاحبتي غادة   ١٠. شجرة صغيرة

الوحدة السابعة
Unit Seven

In this unit:

Letters ف ق ك ل

Vocabulary and Conversation:
Everyday Vocabulary

Culture:
Expressions with الله
Guests' and Hosts' Roles

Letters and Sounds

ف **faa**

This letter is pronounced like *f* as in *feather*.

🎧 **Listening Exercise 1. Reading** ف **(At home)**

Listen to and read aloud the words containing ف.

١. فَرَح	٢. فَرِيد	٣. دَفْتَر
٤. سَفِير	٥. عَفَاف	٦. صُفُوف

🎧 **Writing**

ف   ـف   ـفـ   ف   ف   ـفـ ـف   ـف

ف is a connecting letter with a relatively stable shape. Its independent and final forms have a "tail" that is unusual in that it remains on the line rather than dipping below. Watch and imitate Ustaaz El-Shinnawi as he demonstrates the connecting and nonconnecting shapes, and notice the small size and oval shape of the loops he draws. To write independent ف, begin above the line and draw a flat loop around to your left, up, and down around. Keep the loop of ف small and just above the line, resting on a short "neck." Continue along the line into a hook to finish the tail as Ustaaz El-Shinnawi does. Practice writing independent ف:

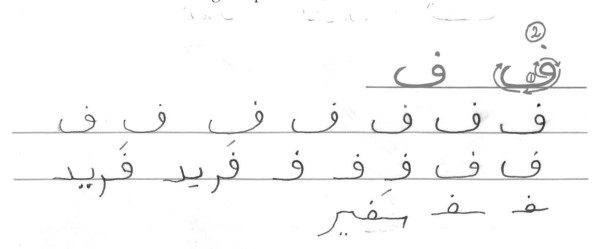

To write ـف in initial position, begin the same way and finish with a connecting segment into the next letter. Copy the word في :

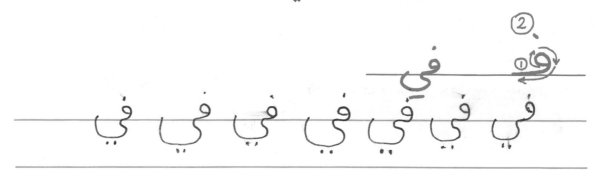

The loop of medial ـفـ is small and oval (it is much smaller than that of ـط and has a different shape). Start from the connecting segment and loop up to your left and back around to the line and into the connecting segment, as the example shows:

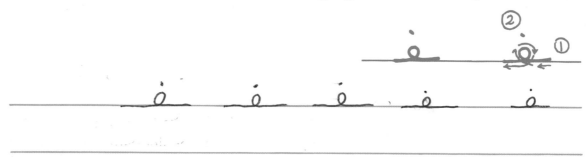

Write صِفـر , copying the example:

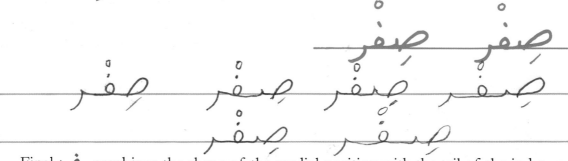

Final ـف combines the shape of the medial position with the tail of the independent ف. Copy صَفّ :

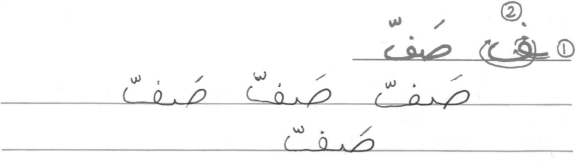

🎧 **Drill 1. Dictation (At home)**

Watch the video and write below the names you hear. Watch and listen as many times as necessary. They are grouped according to gender. Which six are female names and which are male names?

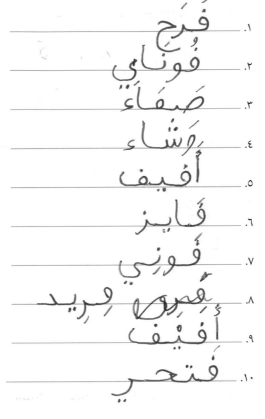

١. فَرَج

٢. فُونَاي

٣. صَفَاء

٤. رِشَاء

٥. أُفِيف

٦. فَايِز

٧. فُوزِي

٨. أُمرو مريد

٩. أُفِيف

١٠. فَتحي

ق qaaf

This letter represents a new sound, the emphatic counterpart to the sound of *k*. Like the other emphatic sounds, it is pronounced with the tongue low in the mouth, and it affects the quality of the surrounding vowels so that fatHa sounds like *u* in *but*. The qaaf is pronounced at the very back of the tongue. Take a minute to become more familiar with this area of your mouth. Open your mouth and say aah, as if you were at a doctor's appointment. Your tongue should be flat in your mouth. Without raising your tongue, pull it back so that the base of your tongue closes off air by pulling back against the throat. The only thing that should move in your mouth is your tongue, and only at the very back, as if you were sliding it back like a sliding door. At this point you should not be able to breathe through your mouth, although it is wide open. Practice doing this first without making a sound. After performing this exercise several times, make a sound by forcefully releasing the air. The result will be the sound ق. Refine your pronunciation by practicing Listening Exercises 2 and 3.

🎧 **Listening Exercise 2. Contrasting ق and ك (At home)**

Listen several times to the contrast between ق and ك in the alphabet videos.

🎧 **Listening Exercise 3. Reading and pronouncing ق (At home)**

Listen to ق in these words and read along:

٣. دَقيـقة   ٢. قارِب   ١. قاف

٦. فِراق   ٥. بَرقـوق   ٤. شَفيـق

🎧 **Drill 2. Hearing ق (At home)**

Listen to the audio to hear nine words. For each, select Yes if you hear ق and select No if you do not.

1. Yes No	2. Yes No	3. Yes No
4. Yes No	5. Yes No	6. Yes No
7. Yes No	8. Yes No	9. Yes No

🎧 **Writing**

ق   ـقـ   ـقـ   قـ   ق

ق is a connector, and its shape is similar to that of ف in its connected positions, except that ق takes two dots above. In independent and final positions, ق takes a deep semicircle tail that drops well below the line like that of س and ص. Watch Ustaaz El-Shinnawi as he writes ق in its various shapes and copy the shapes he draws. Notice that he connects the two dots into a bar, the same way we connect the two dots of ت in handwriting. To write independent ق, make the same loop you made for ف, then drop below the line to draw the tail and make sure to bring the tail all the way back up to the line. Copy the example and the word فَوق *(above)*:

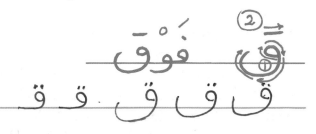

Initial ـق is written just like initial ف, but with two dots run together. Copy the example:

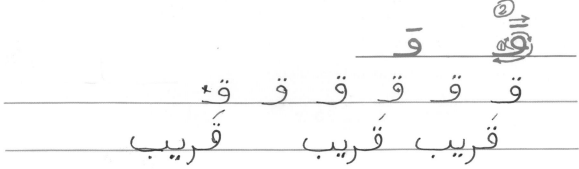

Practice by writing وَرَقة *(paper)*. Do not stop to dot until you have finished writing the word:

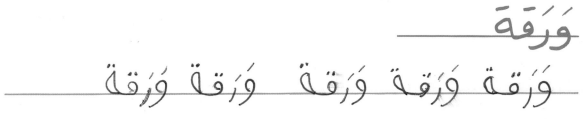

Medial ـقـ has the same shape and size as medial ـفـ and is connected in the same way. Practice by writing دَقيـقـة *(minute)*:

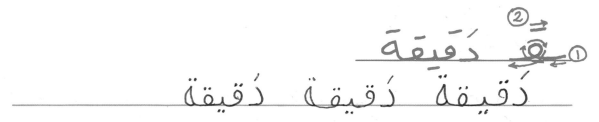

Unlike final ـف , final ـق takes a tail that drops well below the line, just like that of س. Make sure to bring it all the way back up to the line. Practice final ـق by writing رَفيق *(friend, comrade)*:

🎧 **Drill 3. Dictation (At home)**

Watch the video and write below the words you hear, including all vowels. Watch and listen as many times as necessary.

١. أَقارِب	٢. إِبريسِيق	٣. جوڤوق
٤. زوڤاؤ	٥. بَرّوٓق	٦. تابِق

ك kaaf

This letter corresponds to English *k* as in *likewise*.[1] ك represents a familiar sound that takes no extra effort on your part. Take care to distinguish between it and ق, which is pronounced deep in the throat. **Remember:** ق is an emphatic letter that deepens the quality of surrounding vowels, whereas vowels surrounding ك are frontal.

🎧 **Listening Exercise 4. Reading and pronouncing ك (At home)**

Listen to the words containing ك and repeat.

١. كِتاب	٢. دُكتور	٣. حِكاية
٤. أَكيد	٥. شُكوك	٦. رَكيك

---
[1]Note that Arabic ك is never aspirated; that is, it has no "breathy" sound like that of *k* in *kite*.

🎧 Listening Exercise 5. Distinguishing between ق and ك (At home)

Listen to the difference between ك and ق in the pairs of words and repeat:

١. كَدَّس / قَدَّس ٢. رَكيـك / رَقيـق

٣. كابـوس / قابـوس ٤. باكِر / باقِر ٥. شَكّ / شَقّ

🎧 Writing

كك ـك ك ـك ك

As Ustaaz El-Shinnawi demonstrates, ك is a connecting letter that has two distinct shapes, one in independent and final positions, and one in initial and medial positions. To write independent ك, start above the line at the top of the letter, draw straight down to the line, then curve and follow the line. Make a tiny hook at the end, then pick up your pen and draw a little hamza-like figure inside the angle. The shape of this mark, which may have originated as a miniature ک, may vary slightly in different scripts. Copy the word أخبارك:

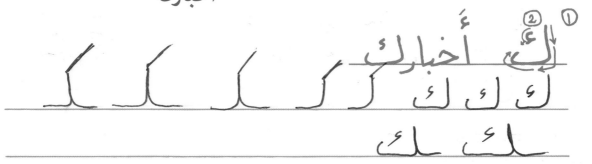

When ک is connected to a letter it has a cross bar on the top; however, this is written last, like the vertical bar of ط and ظ. To write initial ک, start as you do the independent form, drawing down to the line, then make a right angle and draw along it into a connecting segment. Note that the body of initial ک is not exactly perpendicular to the line on the paper—it may be slightly slanted or even curved, depending on individual style. After you finish writing the skeleton of the word, go back and "cross" the ک as shown (it does not matter if the bar is not exactly

lined up, but keep it as close as possible). Copy initial ك, following the arrows:
Now practice writing initial ك in كَبِير *(big, old)*:

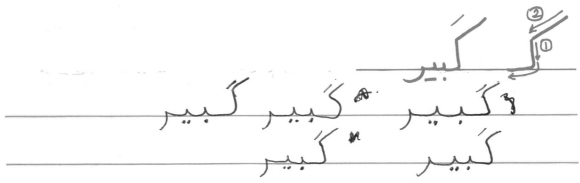

Medial ـكـ is written like initial ك, except that you must start from a connecting segment on the line and draw up, then trace the same line back down. (Again, the body does not have to be exactly perpendicular to the line, and its exact angle may vary somewhat.) Wait until you finish writing the word to draw the cross bar.
Practice writing medial ـكـ in سُكَّر :

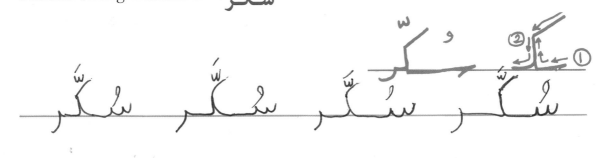

In certain artistic scripts and fonts, initial and medial ك take slightly different shapes. Find ك in each of these words:

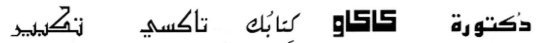

Final ـك is similar in shape to independent ك except that it is connected to the previous letter. Start from the connecting segment, draw a line up that is roughly perpendicular to the line, then trace it back down and give it a flat tail along the line (the same tail you draw for ف). When you have finished writing, give it the little hamza-like mark as in the example:

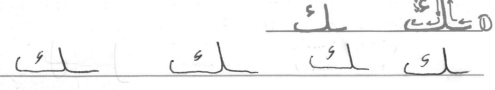

Practice final كـ by writing حَضْرتك :

🎧 **Drill 4. Distinguishing between ق and ك (At home)**

Listen to the audio to hear twelve words, each containing either ق or ك . Select the letter that matches the sound you hear.

1. ق ك   2. ق ك   3. ق ك   4. ق ك   5. ق ك   6. ق ك

7. ق ك   8. ق ك   9. ق ك   10. ق ك   11. ق ك   12. ق ك

🎧 **Drill 5. Reading ق and ك (At-home preparation; in-class activation)**

There are two parts to this exercise:

A. At home, listen and read these pairs of words aloud, and pay attention to ق and ك.

B. In class, take turns with a partner reading a random word and ask your partner to identify it.

	(b)	(a)	
١.	قَادَ	كَادَ	
٢.	شُقـوق	شُكـوك	
٣.	قَسْوة	كَسْوة	
٤.	قَدَّر	كَدَّر	
٥.	حَبَـق	حَبَك	
٦.	بَقَرَ	بَكَرَ	
٧.	صَدَّق	صَدَّكَ	

154

٨. (a) اِكْتِفاء (b) اِقْتِفاء

٩. (a) عِراك (b) عِراق

١٠. (a) كُروش (b) قُروش

🎧 Drill 6. Identifying ق and ك (At home)

Listen to the audio to hear words containing either ق or ك and choose the correct letter to complete the word.

١. ..... ريب ٢. بِطا ..... ة ٣. ص ..... ور

٤. ضَيِّ ..... ٥. اِسْتِشرا ..... ٦. را ..... ص

٧. حَظُّ ..... ٨. فِ ..... رة ٩. سُ ..... ر

🎧 Drill 7. Dictation (At home)

Watch the video and write below the words you hear, including all vowels. Watch and listen as many times as necessary.

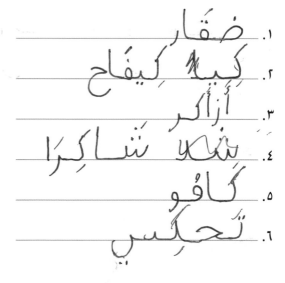

١. ضُقَار

٢. كِبِي كِيفَاح

٣. أَزَأَكِر

٤. ثِكُلا شَاكِرَا

٥. كَاقُو

٦. تَحَكِس

ل laam

This letter represents the sound of the Spanish or French *l*, that is, a frontal *l* in which the front part of the tongue is against the back of the teeth and the tongue is high in the mouth. Americans tend to pronounce *l* with the tongue farther back and lower down in the mouth, resulting in a more emphatic sound than Arabic ل. Say the word *terrible* aloud and notice that the position of your tongue when you say *ble* is similar to the position your tongue holds when you say ص , ض , and ط . To pronounce Arabic ل , hold the tip of your tongue against the back of your teeth at the roof of your mouth and keep your tongue as high and frontal as you can. Maintain this position while repeating the words you hear in Listening Exercise 6.

🎧 Listening Exercise 6. Pronouncing ل

Listen to and repeat the words containing the sound ل, keeping the tip of your tongue against the back of your teeth.

٣. عَالِية   ٢. حَلِيب   ١. لِيبِيا

٧. طَلَعَ   ٦. صَلِيب   ٥. طَوِيل   ٤. حُلُول

🎧 Writing

ـل   ـلـ   لـ   ل

ل is a connecting letter. The shapes of ل are similar to those of ك except that ل has no cross bar and has a narrower and deeper tail that dips below the line in its independent and final positions. Watch Ustaaz El-Shinnawi write the shapes of ل and imitate his movements. Note how similar the shapes of medial ـل (alif) and ـلـ appear: the only difference is that ـلـ connects but alif does not.

To write independent ل , start at the top and draw straight down, continuing below the line into the tail, which should be approximately the same shape as the tail of س, but a little narrower. **The tail must come all the way back up above the line.** Copy the independent shape:

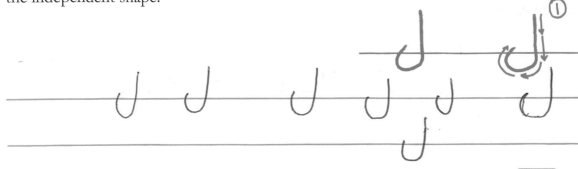

Initial ل is begun the same way, but once you reach the line, curve in to the connecting segment along the line. Write initial ل in ليبيا:

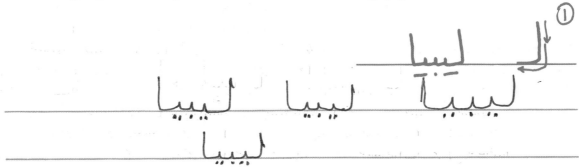

To write medial ـلـ, start from the connecting segment, draw up and then trace back down to the line into the next connecting segment as shown. Practice ـلـ by copying حليب:

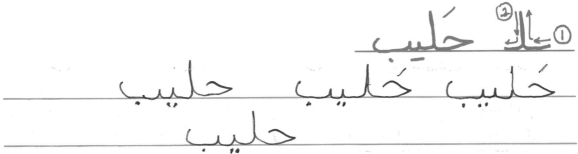

When ل is followed by ح, ج, or خ, its shape is different in handwriting than what you normally see in print. You start writing from the same point but rather than go all the way down to the line, you stop at the height of the خ and curve into it. Copy and practice this shape:

Now copy the following words that begin with ‏الـ‏ *the* (the definite article, which is written connected to the word it modifies):

الجار ‎صباح الخير‎ الحليب

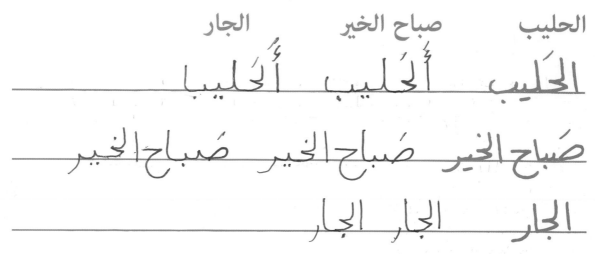

To write final ‏لـ‏ , drop the connecting segment and draw a big, rounded tail. Be sure to dip well below the line and finish the hook by bringing the pen all the way back up to the line again. Practice by writing the word ‏فصل‏ :

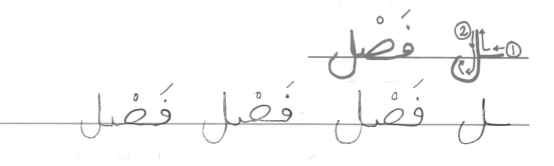

🎧 **Writing**

ﻻ laam alif

The distinct shape ﻻ, the combination of laam followed by alif, must be used to write these two letters wherever they occur in this order in a word. This shape varies slightly in print and handwriting styles. The form you see above is the one you will see in print. In most handwriting styles, however, ﻻ is written in two separate strokes, as Ustaaz El-Shinnawi does. To produce this handwritten form, start as you would to produce the connected ﻝ, but instead of drawing the body straight down, curve it to the left just above the line and **extend** it a little. When you reach the line, pick up your pen and make a slanted alif stroke into the corner of ﻝ as the example shows. Copy the example and write the word ﻻ :

Remember: Alif does not connect to a following letter, therefore, ﻻ **does not connect** to anything following it. Copy and pronounce the following words, and notice where the shadda is placed in the last word in the print form. In handwriting it is written above the ﻻ as usual, but in print, a shadda on ﻻ will often sit to the left.

(students) طُلّاب   (dogs) كِلاب   (children) أَولاد

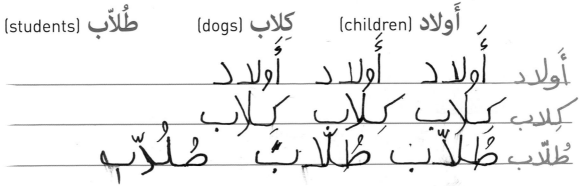

🎧 Drill 8. Dictation (At home)

Watch the video and write below the words you hear, including all vowels. Watch and listen as many times as necessary.

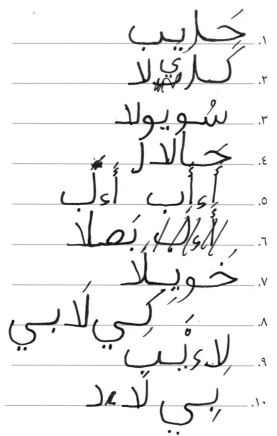

١. حَـلِـيـب

٢. گَارْيِلَا

٣. سُـويُـولِد

٤. حَالَالِد

٥. إِءَاِب أَءَب

٦. لَأَءَاذَ بَصَاد

٧. خُـويَـلِد

٨. گِي لَابِـي

٩. لَءَءَيِـب

١٠. بِـي لَءَد

🎧 **Drill 9. Word recognition** (At home)

Listen to the audio to hear ten words. Select the word you hear in each row.

1.	كَلْب	قَلَب	كِلاب	قَلْب
2.	أضَلّ	أظَلّ	أطَلّ	أذَلّ
3.	عاقِل	عقال	أكل	عَقل
4.	فِقرة	فَكَر	فِكَر	فقر
5.	تَكَلّ	شَكَل	ثَكَل	صَقَل
6.	رگَل	رَفَس	رَكَض	رَقَص
7.	شَرَف	ظَرف	صَرَف	ذَرَف
8.	تَقرير	تكرير	تَكدير	تَقدير
9.	خِزي	حوذي	خُذي	حُزّي
10.	بَلَج	بَلَع	بَلَح	بَلَغ

🎧 **Drill 10. Sound recognition** ذ ص ض ط ظ ع غ (At home)

Listen to the audio to hear fourteen words containing the letters listed above. Choose the letter that correctly completes the word:

١. تَ.....قيـد   ٢. .....رْفة

٣. .....يْف   ٤. فُ.....ور

٥. .....قارِب   ٦. تَ.....ليـل

٧. .....ابِـق   ٨. صـ.....يـر

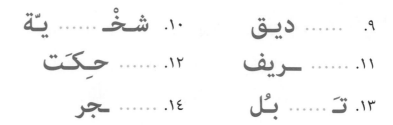

٩. ..... ديق   ١٠. شخْ ..... يّة

١١. ..... ـريف   ١٢. ..... حِكَت

١٣. تَ ..... بُل   ١٤. ..... ـجر

Drill 11. Dictation (At home)

Watch the video and write below the phrases you hear, including all vowels. Watch and listen as many times as necessary. What new words can you add using your knowledge of roots?

٣. _____   ٢. _____   ١. _____

٦. _____   ٥. _____   ٤. _____

Drill 12. Arabic signs (At-home preparation; in-class activation)

Look at the Arabic street signs and sound out the words and names. Which ones do you recognize?

Vocabulary and Conversation: Everyday Vocabulary

🎧 New Vocabulary

Listen to and learn these words:

Meaning	maSri	shaami	Formal /written
page	صَفحة	صَفحة	صَفحة
(piece of) paper	وَرَقة	وَرَقة	وَرَقة
room	اوضة	اوضة	غُرْفة
window	شُبّاك	شِبّاك	شُبّاك
chair	كُرسي	كِرسي	كُرسي
table	طرابيزة	طاولة	طاولة
dog	كَلب	كَلب	كَلب
cat	قُطّة	بِسّة	قِطّة
money	فِلوس	مَصاري maSaari	مال maal
must, need to, have to (fixed form with following verb)	لازِم laazim	لازِم laazim	لازِم laazim
it is possible, can (fixed form with following verb)	مُمكِن mumkin	مُمكِن mumkin	مُمكِن mumkin
nothing	وَلا حاجة	وَلا شي	لا شَيء

Meaning	maSri	shaami	Formal /written
or	وَلّا	وَلّا	أَو
I see (watch)	أَشوف	أَشوف	أُشاهِد ushaahid
you (masc.) see	تِشوف	تشوف	تُشاهِد tushaahid
you (fem.) see	تِشوفي	تشوفي	تُشاهِدين tushaahidiin
he sees	يِشوف	يشوف	يُشاهِد yushaahid
she sees	تِشوف	تشوف	تُشاهِد tushaahid
movie	فيلم film	فيلم film	فيلم film
the cinema, movies	السِّينِما is-sinima	السِّينَما is-sinama	السِّينَما as-sinamaa

🎧 ## Drill 13. Vocabulary matching (At home)

This exercise is on the companion website only. Match the phrases with the pictures you see on your screen.

Drill 14. Vocabulary practice (At-home preparation; in-class activation)

There are two parts to this exercise:

A. Prepare to ask your classmates about what movies they like to see and where. Prepare to answer yourself too. When giving your recommendations, you can use laazim for the "absolute must-see" movies and mumkin for the "possibles."

B. Identify and label as many things in the classroom as you can using scraps of paper or post-it notes. Be sure to describe things as fully as possible with adjectives.

Drill 15. Vocabulary practice (In class)

With a partner, describe this scene of a dorm room above at an Arab university.

🎧 **Drill 16. Listen and interact (At home)**

Someone is going to interview you and will initiate a conversation. Impress the interviewer by responding to the questions with as much Arabic as you can.

Drill 17. Reading aloud (In class)

Read these phrases aloud with a partner. After you finish, make up similar sentences that are personal to you.

١. باب بيتي أبيض

٢. في غرفتي طاولة كبيرة وكرسي صغير

٣. أختي تحبّ تشرب عصير وأخي يحبّ يشرب "بيبسي كولا"

٤. قطّتي تحبّ كلبي

٥. سيارتك كوريّة ؟

٦. في صفحة ٣ أو صفحة ٥ ؟

٧. بيت كبير وفلوس وسيّارة جديدة وحبيبي = ☺

🎧 Drill 18. Scene 7: لازم تشربي حاجة / لازم تشربي شي (At-home preparation; in-class activation)

Watch scene 7:

1. First listen: What is happening?
2. Second listen: What new expressions do you hear this time?
3. Third listen: Plan before you listen this time. Which sections will you focus on and what more do you want to get out of the passage?
4. In class: Discuss with one or two classmates what you noticed in the scene, then listen again together in preparation to act out a similar scene.

🎧 Expressions with Allaah الله

The word for God in Arabic is Allaah. It is used in both formal and spoken contexts with the same formal pronunciation. The word in these two contexts have exact equivalents in meaning, and Christian Arabs and Jewish speakers of Arabic use الله for *God* just like Muslims do. The word الله is used in many everyday expressions that have as much cultural meaning as religious, and are used even by people who are not particularly devout in their faith. It is also not considered offensive to use الله in oaths, as long as one is sincere.

The following are commonly used expressions that contain the word Allaah. It is not always advisable to translate expressions literally because that can obscure culture similarities as well as differences. For example, a literal translation of in shaa' allaah is *If God wills*, but the expression is often used exactly the way an English speaker might use *hopefully*.

English Meaning	Arabic Expression	
Expresses admiration or delight; also (with different intonation) expresses a sudden scare, as when someone almost has an accident	*Allaah!*	الله!
God willing, hopefully	*in shaa' a-llaah*	إن شاء الله
In the name of God (said before or upon beginning something)	*bismi-llaah*	بِسْم الله
Thank God (a positive or neutral response to How are you?); That's good (a positive reaction to news); I have had my fill (a signal that one has finished eating)	*al-Hamdu li-llaah*	الحَمدُ لِلّه
good-bye (Levantine usage)	*Allaah maᶜak*	الله معك
Wow! (when praising or admiring something, or a child, or a success, it expresses sincere good will without a trace of envy)	*maa shaa' a-llaah!*	مـا شـاءَ الله!
There is no God but God (said upon hearing bad news)	*laa ilaaha illa-llah*	لا إله إلا الله

Culture: Guests' and Hosts' Roles

Every culture has its own set of expectations and behaviors involving visiting. In Arab culture, hospitality is a highly prized virtue, and when you visit people at their home or workplace, they will generally insist that you at least have something to drink. The most common items offered are coffee, tea, and soft drinks. If you are invited for a meal, expect to be offered a lot of food, for the hosts will go out of their

way to serve you the most lavish meal they can. They will also keep piling food on your plate and insisting that you eat more! When you have had enough to eat, say *al-Hamdu li-llaah* الـحـمـد لِـلّـه.

You noticed in the video scene that when the host first offered a drink, the guest refused. The initial offer and refusal are somewhat formulaic in Arab culture, and are basically expressions of politeness on both sides. The guest refuses at first because he or she does not want to put the host out, and to show that he or she has not come just to have something to drink. A guest will often refuse several times before accepting. When you are offered something, it is your responsibility not to impose on your host. The offerer will go out of his or her way to be generous but that is not an invitation for you to take advantage of the hospitality. Likewise, when you are entertaining visitors,

remember to fulfill your role as host or hostess by insisting.

After you have read through the expressions and their usage, go to the interactive media to watch scenes where the expressions are used in context. What do you notice? Watch first to understand the context and see how the expressions are being used, then listen again to focus on the pronunciation of the word الله. It is the only word in Arabic whose ل is emphatic in quality without influence from other emphatic consonants. Only when it is preceded by kasra or long vowel ي is الله pronounced with a frontal ل, as you will hear in the expression *bismillaah*.

الوحدة الثامنة
Unit Eight

In this unit:

Letters م ن هـ

More about hamza: آ ؤ ئ

Reading Strategies

Vocabulary and Conversation:
How Are You? States and Feelings

>> Letters and Sounds: Part One

 miim

This letter corresponds to English *m* as in *may*.

 Listening Exercise 1. Recognizing and pronouncing م.

Listen to the words containing م and repeat.

١. مـال   ٢. سَمـير   ٣. مِـصر

٤. جامـعة   ٥. يَوم   ٦. كَلام

 Writing

م is a connecting letter whose basic shape is easily identifiable: a small, round loop. You can see from the words above that the printed forms do not vary much; however, the way the loop is drawn and connected to other letters in handwriting has more varied shapes that take practice to draw and recognize. It is important that you watch Ustaaz El-Shinnawi draw these shapes and practice the direction of the loop in each position until you can write it without needing to stop and check the direction of the loop.

To write independent م , begin on the line and draw a small, round loop over and around to the right, continue along the line a short distance, then make a corner and draw the tail straight down, well below the line. Copy:

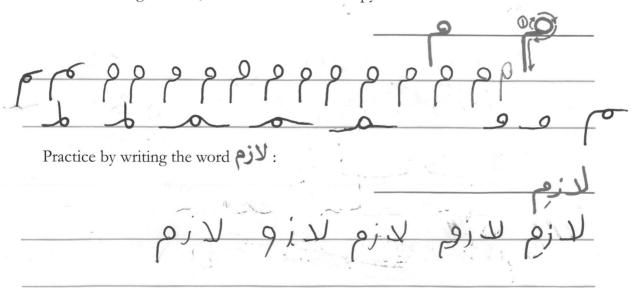

Practice by writing the word لازم :

There are two common styles of writing initial ـم. It may be looped up and over, just like independent م , or looped from underneath in the opposite direction. Once you have closed the loop, continue on into a connecting segment. Choose one to use, then practice by writing the word جامعة :

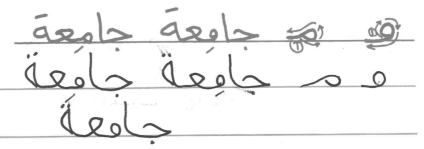

When writing initial ـم followed by ج , ح , or خ , remember to draw the loop well above the line so that you can continue directly into the next letter. Copy the name مَجدي:

Watch Ustaaz El-Shinnawi draw medial ـمـ , which should always loop down from the connecting segment (so that it looks different than the loop of ـفـ). As the examples show, the connecting segment often rests slightly above the line. To practice, copy the words خمسة and حَمّام (bathroom):

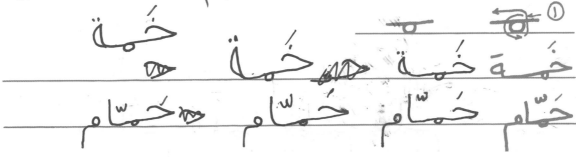

In some typefaces and handwriting styles, ـم may be joined to letters ي, ب, ت, ث, and ـم such that the first letter sits above the medial ـم and drops down into it. Study the print and handwritten examples below and copy the words تمام and مُمتاز *(excellent)*, making sure to loop medial م downward:

(excellent) مُمتاز   تمام

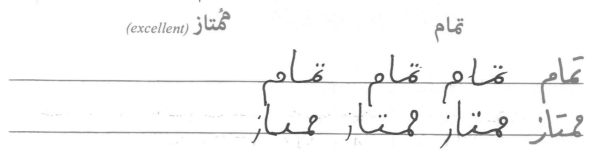

When م follows an initial (unconnected) ل, such as in the definite article ال, it is often written in the corner formed when ل meets the line as Ustaaz El-Shinnawi shows. This shape appears regularly in handwriting and several common print styles as well. Be on the lookout for this combination, especially in print, where ـم often appears as a little bump on the right of ل, as you see in the examples. Practice this shape by writing and sounding out these country names, المَغرِب and المكسيك:

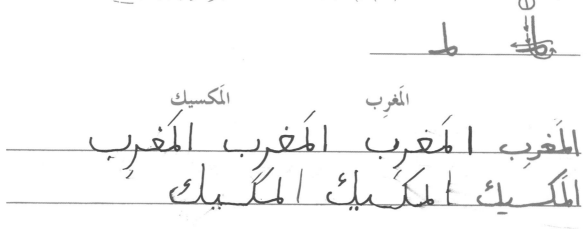

المكسيك   المَغرِب

In handwriting, final ـم must be looped down from the top. Starting from the connecting segment, continue into the loop, then circle down and around to the right, make a full loop, and then continue into the tail. Practice by copying the words قَلَم *(pen; pencil)* and فيلم :

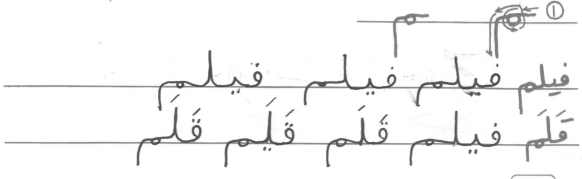

🎧 Drill 1. Dictation (At home)

Watch the video and write below the words you hear. Pay special attention to the shapes of مـ. Watch and listen as many times as necessary.

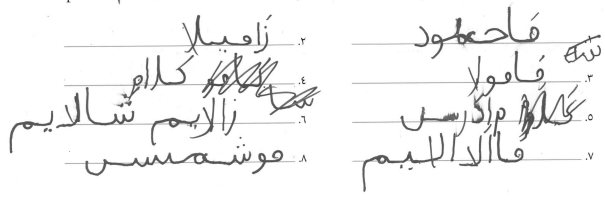

ن nuun

This letter represents the sound *n* as in *noon*.

🎧 Listening Exercise 2. Recognizing ن (At home)

Listen and read aloud words containing ن.

١. نار ٢. لُبـنـان ٣. تونِس ٤. إيران ٥. غَنيّ ٦. سَنة

🎧 Writing

ن   نـ   ـنـ   ـن

ن is a connecting letter whose shape resembles that of ب in initial and medial positions, except for the placement of the dot. It differs from ب in that the independent and final forms of ن take a characteristic tail shape that dips well below the line. Watch

Ustaaz El-Shinnawi and practice drawing the shape of independent ن, making sure to bring the tail back up across the line. Practice the independent shape by copying the word تَعبان *(tired)*:

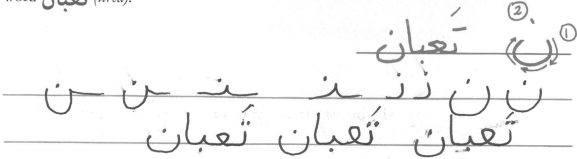

At the beginning or in the middle of a word, write ﻨ as you write ﺒ, but place the dot above rather than below the letter. Practice this shape by copying the phrase أنا وأنت and the word عندك:

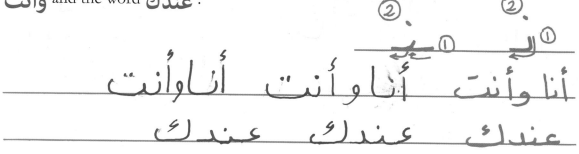

In final position, ﻦ begins with a tooth and then dips immediately into a deep tail below the line. Bring the tail back up across the line. Practice final ن by copying the word اِثنين:

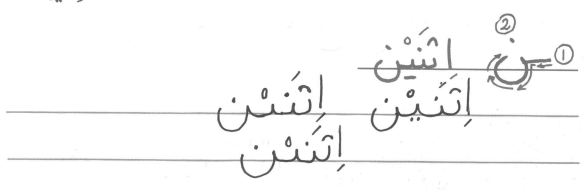

🎧 **Drill 2. Dictation (At home)**

Watch the video and write below the words you hear, including all vowels. Watch and listen as many times as necessary.

٢. حَائِسَان	١. لِلوبِسَان
٤. نَارِيسُ	٣. قَوانِيسُ
٦. نَاشَام	٥. دمَاشَّنون
٨. جونِب	٧. نَاشَام
١٠. هُو موكيْني	٩. بوحِوّم

ه haa

This letter represents a familiar English sound, the one that sounds like the *h* in *house*. Unlike the English *h*, which can be silent, as in *hour*, ـه is always pronounced. In addition, the English *h* sound tends to occur at the beginning of a word or syllable, whereas Arabic ـه can occur in any position. Say "a house," then say those two words as if they were a single word. This is how ـه sounds when it is in the middle of a word. Now say "her," and then say it backwards, pronouncing the *h*. This is how ـه sounds when it occurs at the end of a word. Use this letter (not ح) to write "H" in English proper nouns in Arabic script, such as هارفارد and هيوستن.

🎧 Listening Exercise 3. Recognizing and pronouncing ‎ـهـ‎ (At home)

Listen to and read aloud words containing ‎ـهـ‎.

٣. ظُهُر   ٢. ذَهَب   ١. هَمْزة

٦. بَنـاه   ٥. يَتيه   ٤. نَهْر

🎧 Writing

The forms of this connecting letter vary more than those of any other. In addition, individual style can affect its shape in initial and medial forms. Watch Ustaaz El-Shinnawi and copy his handwriting. The shape ‎ـهـ‎ is the form this letter takes independently and at the beginning of a word. To write this shape, begin slightly above the line and draw a large loop sloping first upward and then downward to your right and back up. This outer loop should be large; its exact shape can vary according to individual style and print type from a pointed to a rounded oval. When you reach the beginning of the loop, continue on, making a small loop **inside** the big one, then continue on down to the line into the connecting segment, making sure that the big loop is closed. Copy the example and practice by writing the word ‎جاهزة‎:

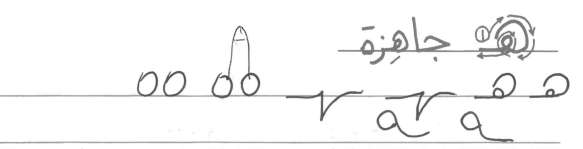

In medial position, ـهـ has two main variations. The first is more common in print: ـهـ (look also at the printed forms of the words in Listening Exercise 3); it consists of two vertical loops, one above and one below the line. The second is more commonly found in handwriting and is written in one stroke as a (more or less) pointed dip below the line. Copy the examples and the words قهوة and سهل *(easy)*:

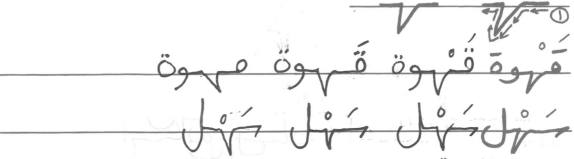

Final ـه takes the same connected and unconnected shapes as ـة except that it has no dots. It is very important to distinguish between these two letters: ـة is a feminine marker; ـه often indicates the possessive *his/its* (masculine). The word الله, for example, is not feminine and is written with ـه, not ـة. To write unconnected final ه, start above the line and draw a loop, just as you drew unconnected ة. Practice with the word عنده:

To write final ـه connected with a previous letter, start from the connecting segment and draw a short line up, then loop around into a flat oval. The exact shape of this oval varies according to individual style and print type. Copy the letter and the word اللّٰه:

The letter ـه occurs regularly at the end of words because it represents the possessive pronoun *his/its*. This ending is pronounced in formal Arabic and is largely silent in spoken Arabic. Practice reading this pronoun and writing final ـه by copying these words:

اِسمُه   أُستاذُه   بَيتُه

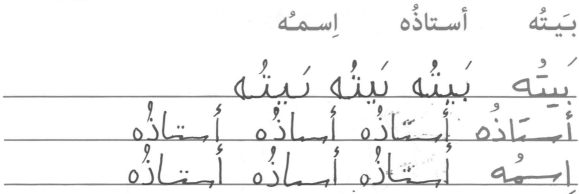

Remember that ـه is a different sound than ح. The sound of ـه corresponds exactly to the sound of English *h* at the beginning of words and syllables, and is very natural for English speakers to pronounce, whereas ح is pronounced deep in the throat and has a slightly raspy sound. You can say ـه without thinking about your throat muscles but you must concentrate to say ح. It is important to distinguish between these two sounds, and this takes practice, so go back to the alphabet chart to watch and listen to these two sounds. The following exercises will also help.

🎧 Listening Exercise 4. Contrasting ـه and ح (At home)

Listen to the contrast between ـه and ح in the following pairs of words:

٢. هُـبوب / حُـبوب   ١. نَـهْر / نَحْر

٥. نَهَـل / نَحَل   ٤. هَمـزة / حَمـزة   ٣. هَل / حَل

٨. بَلَه / بَلَح   ٧. فَهْم / فَحْم   ٦. أبهَر / أبحَر

🎧 **Drill 3. Distinguishing between ‍هـ and ح (At home)**

Listen to the audio to hear twelve words, each containing either ح or ‍هـ. For each word, select the letter that matches the sound you hear.

1.	‍هـ	ح	2.	‍هـ	ح	3.	‍هـ	ح
4.	‍هـ	ح	5.	‍هـ	ح	6.	‍هـ	ح
7.	‍هـ	ح	8.	‍هـ	ح	9.	‍هـ	ح
10.	‍هـ	ح	11.	‍هـ	ح	12.	‍هـ	ح

🎧 **Drill 4. Reading ‍هـ and ح (At-home preparation; in-class activation)**

There are two parts to this exercise:
A. At home, listen and read these pairs of words aloud, and pay attention to ح and ‍هـ.
B. In class, take turns with a partner to read a random word and ask your partner to identify it.

	(a)	(b)
١.	حَول	هَول
٢.	حَمَد	هَمَد
٣.	شَحْم	شَهْم
٤.	جُحود	جُهود
٥.	حافي	هافي
٦.	طَحَل	طَهَل
٧.	أحرَقَ	أهرَقَ
٨.	مُبْحِر	مُبْهِر
٩.	ناحِية	ناهِية
١٠.	اِسْتِحلال	اِسْتِهلال
١١.	إفحام	إفهام
١٢.	أصْحَرَ	أصْهَرَ

🎧 **Drill 5. Distinguishing between** ـه **and** ـح **(At home)**

Listen to the audio to hear words that contain either ـه or ـح and choose the letter that completes the word.

٢. ف .... يم ١. رَ .... بة

٤. ضا .... ك ٣. جَبَ .... ات

٦. ظُ .... ور ٥. لِ .... اف

٨. صَ .... راء ٧. .... رِيّة

١٠. .... ـثالة ٩. أ .... ـم

١٢. .... ـمّام ١١. مـشـ .... ـور

🎧 **Drill 6. Dictation (At home)**

Watch the video and write below the words you hear, including all vowels. Watch and listen as many times as necessary.

١. كَاهـَتـَ

٢. فَجِـحم

٣. حَائَاء

٤. فَوُلُوسحـم

٥. حَائَالِكِلِ

٦. نَطُطَاحِر

Reading Strategies

The reading skill that you have been working on with these materials is that of reading aloud, which focuses on pronunciation and helps you connect sound with image. However, reading aloud does not help with comprehension, because it takes your focus away from the larger context of a sentence or a text. Now that you know the letters of the alphabet, we will begin to work on reading comprehension strategies and skills. These follow the same general pattern as the listening skills you have been developing: first, global comprehension, or the comprehension of general content, then a second reading that focuses on the familiar, and finally close reading, in which you push your comprehension as far as you can. In reading as well as listening, your background knowledge plays an important role in comprehension (you use this skill to read and listen in your native language too).

To develop reading strategies, we will use authentic texts from the real world rather than texts written for student learners. Authentic texts are not meant to be read aloud or to be understood completely. Rather, you will develop important reading strategies such as guessing the meaning of new words from context and using grammatical knowledge to construct meaning. We will begin with the text in Drill 7.

Drill 7. Reading for comprehension (In class)

The first step in reading a text should be a quick "big picture" scan of the text that takes in its layout, distinguishing features, and aspects that will help you answer these kinds of questions: What kind of text is this? What is its larger context? How does that context help me understand what is or might be in the text? Take thirty seconds or so to scan over the text shown and answer: What kind of text is this? What does that tell me about what I might expect to find in it?

On the basis of your answers to these questions, plan your next reading. What am I looking for? What skills do I have that I can put to use here? (At this point, your skills are limited to recognition and sounding out names and words adapted from English, but these will expand soon.) You can assume that this text was chosen because parts of it are accessible to you, so have confidence in your ability to discover what those parts are. Go through the text more carefully now, and look for words that you know or might be able to sound out. When you have finished going through the text for details, take another look at the text as a whole. What more can you say about it now? Share what you have discovered with your classmates.

كل هذا تحت سقف واحد

- أجهزة كمبيوتر، معدات شبكة، نظم تشغيل.
- لاب توب.
- طابعات وحبر ليزر وانكجيت.
- سكانر، بلوترز، مودم.
- برامج أصلية ومعدلة.
- صيانة وتصليح أجهزة الكمبيوتر.
- أنظمة الكابلات.
- صيانة طابعات وسكانر وUPS ... إلخ.
- مشغلات ديسك وسي دي وطاولات كمبيوتر.
- تأجير أجهزة كمبيوتر.
- اكسسوارات أخرى.

المركز الوطني للكمبيوتر

صندوق بريد: ٢٢٦٣ الدوحة - قطر فاكس: ٤٣١٥٠٥٨
E-mail: natcomp@qatar.net.qa • Website: www.nccqatar.com

Letters and Sounds: Part Two

More about همزة

Thus far, you have learned to write ء on an alif seat, or كُرسي, at the beginning of a word as أ, and on the line without a كُرسي at the end of a word as ء. It can also occur in either of these spellings in the middle or at the end of a word. In addition, hamza can be written on two other seats: و and ي (ى with no dots). The rule that hamza is always written on alif at the beginning of the word remains valid. Elsewhere, rules for the writing of hamza depend on the vowels surrounding it.

ئ and ؤ

hamza on kursi ي and kursi و

When hamza occurs in the middle of a word, it may be written on top of alif, or rest on the line, or it may be written on a kursi that has the shape of و, as in ؤ, or ي as in ئ. Just like word-initial alif hamza, in which the alif is not a vowel but a kursi, a و or ي with hamza does not function as a vowel but merely serves as a kursi for hamza.

The choice of seat for ء is determined by the surrounding vowel sounds. When ء occurs in the middle of a word, it may be preceded or followed by any of the vowel sounds, short or long. The kursi of the hamza matches the vowel that precedes or follows according to a hierarchy of vowel sounds: kasra or long vowel ي is the strongest vowel sound, followed by Damma or long vowel و, and in last place, fatHa or alif. The general principle at work here is that hamza is written on the kursi that matches the strongest vowel sound on either side of it. Whenever hamza in the middle of a word is immediately preceded or followed by a kasra or long vowel ـي, hamza is written on a ى seat: ئ or ـئ. **Remember**: when ى serves as a kursi for hamza, it takes no dots.

🎧 Listening Exercise 5. Reading ـئ (At home)

Listen to the following words containing ـئ and repeat. Look and listen for the kasra immediately preceding or following hamza:

١. طائِرة   ٢. عائشة   ٣. خائِب

٤. قائِل   ٥. أسْئِلة   ٦. قارِئ   ٧. طوارِئ

Practice writing and reading by copying and sounding out these words:

شاطئ   قَبائِل   طائِرات   سُئِلَ   رَئيس

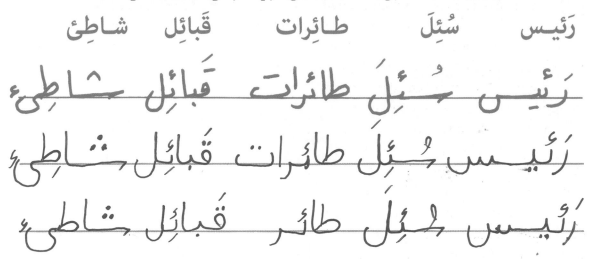

If neither kasra nor ي precedes or follows hamza, but there is instead a Damma or long vowel و, the hamza is written on a و seat: ؤ .

🎧 Listening Exercise 6. Reading ؤ (At home)

Listen to the following words containing ؤ and repeat. Notice the Damma and/or و on either side of it:

١. فُؤاد   ٢. سُؤال   ٣. رُؤوس

٤. رَؤوف   ٥. بُؤْس   ٦. يؤْسِف

Practice writing and reading ؤ by copying and sounding out these words:

يُؤْمِن   مُؤْلِم   تَفاؤُل   سُؤال

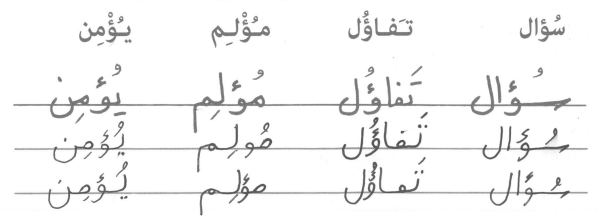

In other cases, that is, when medial **هَـمْـزة** is surrounded by fatHa or alif, it is written on alif, as you learned earlier, except when it follows alif, in which case it rests on the line and takes no **كرسي**. You can remember this by noting that Arabic does not allow two alifs to be written together. You do not need to memorize all the rules for writing hamza right away; for now you are expected to recognize the seats of hamza when you see them and learn to pronounce and write correctly words containing hamza one by one. The most important thing to remember is that the **و** and **ى** with hamza, like the alif in alif hamza, are not vowels and have no sound of their own. The only sound is that of the hamza itself.

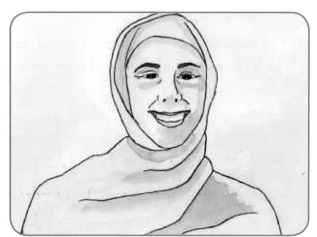

أَلِـف مَـدَّة آ

What happens when **هَـمْـزة** is followed by the long vowel alif? The Arabic word al-Qur'aan is one word that contains this combination. In this word, the consonant **هَـمْـزة** is part of the root, and it is followed by an alif. This combination can occur at the beginning or in the middle of a word, and in each case it is spelled in the same way, with the symbol **آ** , which represents **ا** + **ء** (hamza + alif). This symbol is called **مَـدَّة** madda, which means lengthening, and it can only occur on alif. The alif madda is pronounced as hamza followed by long vowel alif. It is important to pronounce both the hamza and the alif when reading alif madda. Practice this in Listening Exercise 7.

🎧 **Listening Exercise 7. Hearing and reading آ (At home)**

Listen to words containing آ and repeat:

٣. آكُل	٢. آمين	١. آن
٦. مِـرآة	٥. الآن	٤. القُرآن

Writing

آ

The مَـدّة sign is written on top of the **الف** as a slightly wavy line just above it. Watch Ustaaz El-Shinnawi and copy the example and the word **القـرآن**:

Practice writing the sentence **أنا آسِف/آسِفة** (choose your gender):

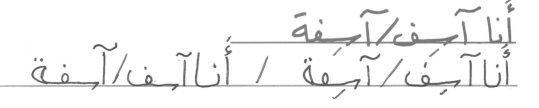

🎧 **Drill 8. Word recognition**

Listen to the audio to hear twelve words. Circle the word you hear in each row.

١.	زأر	زار	ذعر
٢.	فرع	قرع	فزع
٣.	غلاب	كلاب	قلاب
٤.	صورة	سورة	ثورة
٥.	عرف	عرك	عرق
٦.	خائب	غائب	عائب
٧.	تفاؤل	تفاعل	تفاءل
٨.	سعل	سأل	شعل
٩.	قباب	كباب	ضباب
١٠.	سائر	ثائر	شاعر
١١.	سر	صر	زر
١٢.	قبس	كبس	جبس

🎧 **Drill 9. Letter connection (At home)**

Connect the letters to form words, then listen and write the vowels you hear:

١. ت + س + ا + ؤ + ل = _____

٢. ظ + ر + و + ف + ي = _____

٣. و + ظ + ي + ف + ة = _____

٤. أ + ك + ل + ا + ت = _____

٥. غ + ر + ا + ئ + ب = _____

٦. ج + ح + ا + ف + ل = _____

٧. ف + و + ا + ئ + د = _____

٨. إ + ف + ر + ي + ق + ي + ا = _____

٩. خ + ل + ي + ف + ة = ــــــــــــــــــــــــ

١٠. ض + ر + و + ر + ا + ت = ــــــــــــــــــــــــ

١١. أ + ظ + ا + ف + ر + ي = ــــــــــــــــــــــــ

١٢. أ + ن + هـ + ا + ر = ــــــــــــــــــــــــ

١٣. ك + ر + ي + م = ــــــــــــــــــــــــ

١٤. م + ذ + ا + هـ + ب = ــــــــــــــــــــــــ

١٥. ط + م + ا + ط + م = ــــــــــــــــــــــــ

١٦. ن + هـ + ا + ي + ا + ت = ــــــــــــــــــــــــ

١٧. ك + ل + ا + م + هـ = ــــــــــــــــــــــــ

١٨. أ + ا + ك + ل + هـ + ا = ــــــــــــــــــــــــ

١٩. ك + هـ + ر + ب + ا + ء = ــــــــــــــــــــــــ

٢٠. ت + ع + ظ + ي + م = ــــــــــــــــــــــــ

٢١. غ + ف + ر + ا + ن = ــــــــــــــــــــــــ

٢٢. أ + س + ئ + ل + ة = ــــــــــــــــــــــــ

ممنوع الانتظار

ممنوع الدخول

ممنوع الوقوف

>> Vocabulary and Conversation: How Are You? States and Feelings

 ### New Vocabulary

Listen to and learn these words. Remember that masculine and feminine words are sometimes given in the same place:

Meaning	maSri	shaami	Formal /written
(that) means, that is	يَعني	يَعني	يَعني
building	عِمارة	بِناية	بِناية
office, desk	مَكتَب	مَكتَب	مَكتَب
library; bookstore	مَكتَبة	مَكتَبة	مَكتَبة
word	كِلمة	كِلمة	كَلِمة
sentence	جُملة	جِملة	جُملة
test, examination	إمتِحان	إمتِحان	إمتِحان
pen or pencil	قَلَم	قَلَم	قَلَم
drill, exercise	تَمرين	تَمرين	تَمرين
bathroom, toilet	الحَمّام؛ التواليت	الحَمّام؛ التواليت	الحَمّام
close to, near (masc./fem.)	قُرَيِّب/ة مِن	قَريب/ة مِن	قَريب/ة مِن
far from (masc./fem.)	بِعيد/ة عَن	بْعيد/ة عَن	بَعيد/ة عَن
tired	تَعبان/ة	تَعبان/ة	تَعبان/ة
cold	بَردان/ة	بَردان/ة	بَردان/ة
hot	حَرّان/ة	مِشَوِّب/ة	حَرّان/ة

Meaning	maSri	shaami	Formal /written
thirsty	عَطشان/ة	عَطشان/ة	عَطشان/ة
hungry	جَعان/ة	جيعان/ة	جَوْعان/ة
upset (angry or sad)	زَعلان/ة	زَعلان/ة	زَعلان/ة
exhausted	خَلْصان/ة	-	-
happy	مَبسوط/ة	مَبسوط/ة	سَعيد/ة
sick	عَيّان/ة	مَريض/ة	مَريض/ة ⨍⨍
a little	شوَيّة	شوَيّ؛ شوَيّة	قَليلاً qaliilan
What's wrong (with you)?	مالَك/مالِك؟	شوبَك/شوبِك؟	ما بِكَ / ما بِكِ؟
Feel better! Get well soon!	سَلامتَـك!	سَلامتِـك!	-
(response to) سلامتك!	الله يِسَلِّمَـك	الله يِسَلِّمَـك	-

🎧 Drill 10. Vocabulary matching (At home)

This exercise is on the companion website only. Match the phrases with the pictures you see on your screen.

Drill 11. Vocabulary practice (At-home preparation; in-class activation)

Print out or draw a map of your campus and label it in Arabic as much as you can to help any Arabic-speaking people who might visit your school. In class, with a partner, prepare a brief presentation on the places you identified, and say as much as you can about them in Arabic.

Drill 12. Vocabulary practice (In class)

With a partner, describe the scene shown above in as much detail and with as much imagination as you can.

🎧 Drill 13. "izzayyak?" (At home)

Watch the cartoon " ازّيّك؟ "
What new words and expressions do you hear?
What is the Egyptian word that means "very"?

🎧 Drill 14. Vocabulary matching (At home)

This exercise is on the companion website only. You will see pictures showing Layla in her many moods and emotional states, and you will hear words that describe them. Match each word you hear to the picture that represents it.

🎧 Drill 15. Scene 8: سلامتك ! (At-home preparation; in-class activation)

Watch scene 8 using the listening steps and strategies you have learned.
What expression and response do you hear in this kind of situation?
In class, act out situations with your classmates in which you might use this expression.

الوحدة التاسعة
Unit Nine

In this unit:

The Definite Article الـ

Names of Arab Countries

Vocabulary and Conversation: Describing People

Culture: مَعْلِـهْـش! :Culture

Roots and Patterns

>> Letters and Sounds

أَلِف لام الـ

Called أَلِف لام in Arabic after the names of the letters, the segment الـ represents the definite article in Arabic, similar to *the* in English. Compare these two pairs of nouns:

كتاب (a book)   الكتاب (the book)

أستاذ (a teacher)   الأستاذ (the teacher)

These examples show that الـ makes an indefinite noun definite. Of course, the usage of Arabic الـ is not exactly equivalent to that of English *the*. For example, you have already learned how to say جامعة القاهرة (*The University of Cairo*), in which جامعة is definite although it does not have الـ. You will learn more about the usage of الـ over the next few weeks; in the meantime, **remember that a word with الـ is always definite**.

Proper nouns are definite whether or not they begin with الـ; for example, مصر , فَرَنسا , إيطاليا is definite, as are سوريا تونس . Non-Arabic names, such as أمريكا and , generally do not take الـ . The names of Arab cities and countries must be memorized because there is no rule that determines whether or not they take الـ . For example, بيروت دِمَشق and do not take الـ , but القاهرة does.

🎧 Listening Exercise 1. Listening for الـ

Listen to these words with and without الـ

١. بيت / البيت   ٢. قلم / القلم

٣. مكتب / المكتب   ٤. أستاذة / الأستاذة

٥. مكتبة / المكتبة   ٦. كرسي / الكرسي

Pronunciation of ‫الـ‬

Long before you learned to write ‫الـ‬, you learned the greetings ‫صباح النّور‬ and ‫السّلام عليكم‬. In both ‫السّلام‬ (as-salaam) and ‫النّور‬ (an-nuur), we do not hear or pronounce the ‫لـ‬, but rather the letters ‫س‬ and the ‫ن‬ each take a shadda, which is the result of ‫لـ‬ becoming assimilated into or "swallowed by" those consonants. The letters ‫س‬ and ‫ن‬ belong to a group of letters called ‫الـحُروف الـشَّمسيّة‬, *sun letters*, which assimilate or swallow the ‫لـ‬ of ‫الـ‬. The name sun letters comes from the Arabic word ‫شَمس‬ (sun) because ‫ش‬ is one of the letters that behaves in this way. The shadda on the shamsi letters reflects the "length" of the assimilated ‫لـ‬ added to the length of the letter itself, thus maintaining the length of two consonants with the sound of one.

Contrast the pronunciation of ‫السّلام‬ and ‫النّور‬ with that of ‫صباح الخير‬ in ‫الخير‬. The ‫لـ‬ maintains its pronunciation in ‫الخير‬ because ‫خ‬ belongs to the other group of consonants, ‫الـحُروف القَمَريّة‬. This group of consonants is named after the word ‫قَمَر‬ *moon*, since ‫ق‬ is one of the consonants that do not assimilate the ‫لـ‬ of ‫الـ‬.

The following chart lists the letters in their proper classes. Of course, you cannot carry the chart around with you, so you must memorize which letters are shamsi and which are qamari. You can, however, use pronunciation as a guide. Pronounce each of the shamsi letters out loud and pay attention to where your tongue is placed. For all of these letters, the tip of the tongue is at or near the back of your teeth at the roof of your mouth, which is the same position it is placed for the pronunciation of ‫لـ‬. The qamari letters, on the other hand, are pronounced with the tongue in various other positions. With a little bit of practice you should be able to identify the shamsi letters just by pronouncing them.

‫الحروف الشمسية:‬	‫ت ث د ذ ر ز س ش ص ض ط ظ ل ن‬
‫الحروف القمرية:‬	‫أ ب ج ح خ ع غ ف ق ك م هـ و ي‬

🎧 Listening Exercise 2. Recognizing *sun* and *moon* letters

Listen to these words that contain *sun* and *moon* letters and repeat, and pay special attention to the pronunciation of ‫الـ‬:

الحُروف القَمَريـة:

١. البيـت ٢. القلم ٣. الأستاذ ٤. الكتاب ٥. الأوتوبيـس

الحُـروف الشَـمسيَّـة:

١. الشّارع ٢. السّيّارة ٣. الصّفّ ٤. الطّاولة ٥. الطّائرة

Note that each word in the first group of words contains the sound ل , whereas in the second group, you do not hear ل , but rather a shadda on the following consonant. This shadda is sometimes written in, as it is above, as a reminder of correct pronunciation. In fully vocalized texts it is considered part of proper vowelling and will always be written in. It is a good idea to write the shadda on shamsi letters as a reminder of correct pronunciation.

🎧 Drill 1. Reading ال aloud (At home)

Practice reading aloud words with ال . First, identify which words have shamsi letters and which have qamari letters without looking at the chart. Write shadda on each shamsi letter and sukuun on the ل before each qamari letter as in the examples, then read the word aloud and check your pronunciation with the audio.

Examples: الرّاديو / القْلم

٣. المدينة	٢. البيْت	١. الدكتور
٦. الكَعبة	٥. الشارع	٤. الطائِرة
٩. القُرآن	٨. الديمُقراطي	٧. الصفّ
١٢. العَيْن	١١. اللَوح	١٠. السـيارة
١٥. النَهر	١٤. السؤال	١٣. الغَزال
١٨. الحِزب	١٧. الإسلام	١٦. الظَلام
	٢٠. الثَقافة	١٩. الخَير

🎧 Drill 2. Recognizing ‏ال‎ on words (At home)

Listen to the audio to hear twelve words. Select Yes for each word that has ‏ال‎ and select No for each word that does not. Remember to listen for shadda on shamsi letters.

1. Yes No	2. Yes No	3. Yes No	4. Yes No
5. Yes No	6. Yes No	7. Yes No	8. Yes No
9. Yes No	10. Yes No	11. Yes No	12. Yes No

🎧 Drill 3. Word recognition (At home)

Listen to the audio to hear ten words, and then select the word you hear in each row. Pay special attention to the first syllable in each word and listen for the presence or absence of shadda on *sun* letters.

أسلم	إسلام	١. السلام
أصفّ	صفّ	٢. الصفّ
أعمل	عمل	٣. العمل
أنهاية	نهاية	٤. النهاية
أقلام	قلم	٥. القلم
أصوم	صوم	٦. الصوم
أصبح	صباح	٧. الصباح
أظلم	ظلام	٨. الظلام
أثاني	ثاني	٩. الثاني
أنور	نور	١٠. النور

Once you have learned to identify ال on individual words, start listening for it in phrases and sentences. In normal speech, word boundaries are often elided and it can be difficult to determine where one word ends and the next begins. Listening for ال helps you to hear word boundaries. Along with the sound of ل that you will hear on qamari letters, you need to develop an ear for the shadda on shamsi letters. Practice this in Drill 4.

🎧 Drill 4. Listening for ال and word boundaries in phrases (At home)

Listen to the audio to hear eight phrases. Determine where the word boundary is and whether the second word in each is definite or indefinite. Select Yes if the second word is definite and select No if the second word is indefinite.

1. **Yes** No	2. **Yes** No	3. **Yes** No	4. **Yes** No
5. **Yes** No	6. **Yes** No	7. **Yes** No	8. **Yes** No

Drill 5. Reading ال (In class)

Read aloud the following words and pay special attention to ال and shamsi letters:

٤. الخَضْراء	٣. الدرس	٢. الطالب	١. البناية
٨. النـور	٧. القطّة	٦. الكـلب	٥. الـزَعَل
١٢. الامتحان	١١. الضـابِط	١٠. اللازم	٩. الساعة
١٦. الحمّام	١٥. المكتبة	١٤. الـورقة	١٣. الحلـيب
٢٠. الشبّاك	١٩. التمرين	١٨. الصفحة	١٧. السـيّارة
٢٤. اليَمَـن	٢٣. الذَهـاب	٢٢. الظَبي	٢١. الغـرفة
٢٨. القلـم	٢٧. الثاني	٢٦. الجامعة	٢٥. الـرَجُل
	٣٠. الصحيح	٢٩. العَفو	

🎧 **Drill 6. Dictation (At home)**

Watch the video and write below the words you hear, including all vowels. Remember to listen for الـ according to the rules you have learned. Watch and listen as many times as necessary.

٢. النَّجَار	١. النِّثْرابُ
٤. قالا	٣. أَسْماء
٦. أَلجِرَّفَة	٥. أَطاباح
٨. أَطالَنمة	٧. أَطايَارُ
١٠. لِلْحايِر	٩. أُطْجِير
١٢. أُظْواءٌ	١١. الله إِسِية

هَمْزة الوَصل أ

You have seen that words like أُستاذ begin with the consonant هَمْزة, even if hamza is not always written in unvowelled texts. It is the هَمْزة that "allows" you to pronounce the vowel that follows it. In most words that begin with هَمْزة, the vowel that the hamza carries always remains the same; for example, أُخت and أخ are always pronounced the same way. However, the هَمْزة of ال is a special kind of hamza called هَمْزة الوَصل, which means "elidable hamza". "Elidable" means that, when preceded by another word, the hamza and its vowel drop in both pronunciation and writing. In writing, the symbol waSla وَصلة takes the place of the هَمْزة, and in pronunciation, the original vowel on the alif is swallowed by the final vowel of a previous word or by a "helping vowel:" a short vowel that allows you to link the two words together without pausing. Thus, in the case of ال, the fatHa vowel on the alif is not pronounced (unless it is the first word in the sentence). This happens whenever a noun or adjective with ال occurs in noun phrases and prepositional phrases. Compare the pronunciation of ال in two different sentence positions:

١. (al-bayt jadiid)   البيت جديد

٢. (akhii fi l-bayt)   أخي في البيت

You will hear examples of this elision in Listening Exercise 3. Practice aloud with the audio until you can pronounce the phrases smoothly.

🎧 Listening Exercise 3. Eliding ال in prepositional phrases (At home)

Listen carefully to ال in the second word of each phrase. You will not hear the ا of the ال because it is swallowed by the final vowel of the preceding word:

٢. أمريكا ٱللاتينية   ١. أبي ٱلعزيز

٤. في ٱلجامعة   ٣. في ٱلبيت

٦. مدرّسو ٱلجامعة   ٥. بيتي ٱلجديد

٨. كرسي ٱلطالب   ٧. والدا ٱلبنت

🎧 Writing

أ

The symbol for **همزة الوصل**, called **وَصلة**, is not normally written except in completely vowelled texts. It can only occur at the beginning of a word, and the overwhelming majority of cases occur on **الـ**. Practice writing it by copying the example:

🎧 Drill 7. Identifying **همزة** and **وصلة** (At home)

Listen and watch as the following phrases are read aloud. Some will contain regular **همزة** or **وصلة** and some will contain **همزة الوصل**. Mark either **همزة** according to what you hear:

٢. مع الشاي	١. والـدي استاذ
٤. لي اسنان	٣. عنـدي الم
٦. أين البيت ؟	٥. صديقي الفرنسي
٨. في المدينة	٧. هُـوَ احمد
١٠. أنا الاستاذ	٩. أخو البنت

Drill 8. Using ال in phrases (In class)

Work with a partner to create as many short sentences as you can with definite nouns and the prepositions listed below. A few nouns are also suggested as prompts to get you started, but do not be limited by those you see here. The prepositions are listed by function, which is a more helpful way to remember them than by translation. Prepositions do not translate well across languages, and Arabic is no exception. Arabic also treats human nouns differently than nonhuman nouns in some ways; note that the meaning "with" in Arabic is expressed differently depending on whether the action involves doing something "with" another person, or "with" an instrument, such as a pen, including coffee "with" milk and sugar.

١. مِن from (a source or place of origin)

٢. في in, at (location in time and space)

٣. بـ "with" (things, such as an instrument)

٤. مَعَ with (people)

As you form your sentences, keep in mind two points:

1. Remember to elide the fatHa in ال so that the end of the previous word carries right into the laam or (if the consonant is a shamsi letter), the shadda.

Most prepositions end in a vowel but in the case of مِن, which does not, we need to add a helping vowel. Formal Arabic uses fatHa: مِنَ البَيت, whereas spoken Arabic generally uses a schwa.

2. The preposition بـ is written attached to the following word (this is a rule for all one-letter words): بالحليب

Nouns to get you started:

الصفّ / الجامعة / الشارع / المكتبة / الاستاذ / الشاي / القطّة / السيّارة / الامتحان / البناية / البيت / القلم / الرّاديو

Examples:

أختي في البيت / عندي امتحان مع الأستاذ

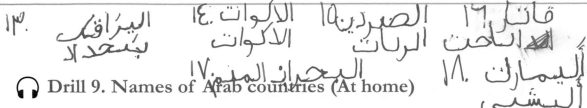

Drill 9. Names of Arab countries (At home)

Look at the map of the countries where Arabic is spoken in everyday life. Listen to the names and capitals of each country in Arabic. Then, write the names out in Arabic.

Drill 10. Reading comprehension (In class)

Key word: engineering الهَندَسة

Use the reading strategies listed below that you learned in unit 8 to read the following text.

1. Do the thirty-second scan: What kind of text is this? What expectations do you have about its content?

2. Look for the things you expect to see. As you find them, adjust your expectations and focus your search.

3. One section of the text has some English that might provide a clue. Based on that clue, what else can you look for in that section?

4. What new words did you learn from this text by guessing from root or context? What can you figure out about the words **معهد** and **ولاية**?

برامج الهندسة في الدراسات الجامعية الأولى

تم تطوير هذه اللائحة من مقال مجلة "يو اس نيوز وورلد ريبورت":أفضل الجامعات والموقع الإلكتروني StudentReview.com، والتي تم تجميعها على يد طلاب الدراسات العليا في معهد مساتشوسيتس للتكنولوجيا.

جامعة كورنل ، ولاية نيويورك

جامعة جونز هوبكنز ، ولاية ماريلاند

معهد مساتشوسيتس للتكنولوجيا ، ولاية مساتشوسيتس

جامعة ولاية بنسلفانيا ، ولاية بنسلفانيا

جامعة بيردو ، ولاية انديانا

معهد رينسلير بولي تكنيك ، ولاية نيويورك

جامعة رايس ، ولاية تكساس

جامعة ستانفورد ، ولاية كاليفورنيا

جامعة تكساس أي أند أم في كوليج ستايشن ، ولاية تكساس

جامعة الينوي في أوربانا-شامباين ، ولاية الينوي

معهد فرجينيا بولي تكنيك وجامعة ولاية فرجينيا ، ولاية فرجينيا

Vocabulary and Conversation: Describing People

🎧 New Vocabulary

Listen to and learn these words.

Meaning	maSri	shaami	Formal /written
man	راجِل	رِجّال	رَجُل
woman	سِتّ	مَرَة	اِمرأة
girl	بِنت	بِنت	بِنت
boy	وَلَد	وَلَد	وَلَد
story	قِصّة	قُصّة	قِصّة
short (masc./fem.)	قُصَيَّر/ة	قَصير/ة	قَصير/ة
tall, long (masc./fem.)	طَويل/ة	طَويل/ة	طَويل/ة
beautiful (masc./fem.)	جَميل/ة حِلو/ة	حِلو/ة	جَميل/ة
nice, pleasant (masc./fem.)	لَطيف/ة	لَطيف/ة	لَطيف/ة
never mind! Don't worry about it! sorry!	مَعلِهش!	معليش!	-
problem	مُشكِلة	مِشكلة	مُشكِلة
wrong, a mistake	غَلَط	غَلَط	غَلَط
sir/madam (Egyptian only)	أفَندِم	-	-

🎧 Drill 11. Vocabulary matching (At home)

You will hear phrases that contain words you have learned. After each phrase, click on the picture that best represents it.

Drill 12. Vocabulary activation (At-home preparation; in-class activation)

Use your imagination and the new and old vocabulary to write or talk about the people you see in the picture using as many different words as you can.

🎧 Drill 13. Listen and interact (At home)

You are not feeling well today and a friend calls you. Respond to your friend's questions about how you are feeling using as much Arabic as you can.

🎧 Drill 14. Arabic signs (At-home preparation; in-class activation)

Read the Arabic signs and sound out the words and names. Which ones do you recognize?

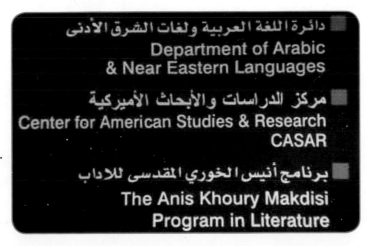

دائرة اللغة العربية ولغات الشرق الأدنى
Department of Arabic & Near Eastern Languages

مركز الدراسات والأبحاث الأميركية
Center for American Studies & Research CASAR

برنامج أنيس الخوري المقدسي للاداب
The Anis Khoury Makdisi Program in Literature

🎧 **Drill 15. Scene 9: ألو (At-home preparation; in-class activation)**

Watch scene 9 using the strategies you have learned, then prepare to act out similar situations in class using the new expressions.

Culture: مَعْلِـهْـش !

The colloquial expression مَعْلِهْش (also spelled معليش; in some eastern dialects, pronounced ما عليه) has a wide range of usages, including calming someone down, consoling someone, and telling someone not to worry. Similar expressions in English include *"never mind"*, *"don't worry about it"*, *"it doesn't matter"*, and *"it's okay"*. In Egypt, it is sometimes used to express *"sorry!"* to excuse a minor lapse, such as an inadvertent bump or late arrival.

In Arab culture, if someone is visibly upset, those nearby will usually try to soothe or calm him or her down, and will most likely try to find out what the problem is even if they do not know the person well. This behavior is not seen as interference but rather as helping to make the situation better and showing proper concern toward one's fellow human beings.

Roots and Patterns

Recognizing Patterns

You have seen that Arabic words are usually formed from a core of three consonants that constitute its basic meaning, called the root of the word. Words are formed by putting roots into different patterns, or syllable structures. To see how this works, let us examine the following adjectives you know, all of which share the same pattern. First, pick out the root of each word and underline the three consonants that comprise it.

قَصير   طَويل   صَغير   كَبير   لَطيف   جَميل

What you are left with after isolating the root are two syllables, the first with a fatHa and the second with long vowel ـي . This syllabic pattern is common among basic adjectives. Recognizing this pattern helps you in two ways: first, for reading comprehension; if you come across an unfamiliar word with this pattern, you can predict that it might be an adjective, and that may help you guess the meaning from context. Second, it will help you predict the pronunciation of similarly shaped words. Try this out by looking at the following sentence:

أشرب قهوة ثقيلة في الصباح وقهوة خفيفة في المساء .

Using what you have learned about patterns, what can you say about the two new words in this sentence? What do you think they mean?

All Arabic nouns, adjectives, and verbs follow sets of patterns that you will learn gradually as you acquire more vocabulary. (At this stage, it is easier to learn a specific word or group of words first and then learn their pattern rather than the other way around.) Plurals in Arabic also follow this pattern system, and Listening Exercise 4 will give you an idea of what plurals look like in Arabic. Some take a suffix, while others rearrange their root in new syllable patterns. Start now to familiarize yourself with these patterns so that you have a head start on memorizing them.

🎧 Listening Exercise 4. Plural patterns of nouns (At-home)

Listen to the following pairs of singular and plural nouns:

٢. مَكتَب / مَكاتِب	١. رَجُل / رِجال
٤. مَكتَبة / مكتبات	٣. بِنت / بَنات
٦. غرفة / غُرَف	٥. ولد / أولاد
٨. بِناية / بنايات	٧. قَلَم / أقلام
١٠. شُبّاك / شَبابيك	٩. فيلم / أفلام

Roots and the Arabic Dictionary

In addition to helping you guess the meaning of new words whose roots you recognize, knowing the root of a word is essential in order to use an Arabic dictionary. Take a look at the Arabic–English glossary if you have not already done so, and notice that the words are not in the alphabetical order you might expect. Arabic dictionaries are not arranged alphabetically by spelling but rather by root. To find a word, you must first identify the root.

Identifying roots is easy in many words, such as in قلم , كتاب , and أشرب. Other words, however, have consonants that are part of the pattern, not the root, such as the plural ending ات you saw above. In the word مكتبة , the prefix مَـ is part of the pattern of the word and not the root, so if we eliminate مـ and the feminine marker ة , we are left with the root ك – ت – ب. In the glossary, then, you should find the words كتاب and مكتبة listed together (in a real dictionary, they would be under the same main entry, ك – ت – ب). In addition to the prefix مَـ, the letter ت is often part of the pattern and not the root, so if you have more than three consonants and one of them is ت , try eliminating the ت . Sometimes identifying the root might take a bit of trial and error. We will return to roots and patterns again and learn more about how they work. In the meantime, practice finding words in drill 16.

Drill 16. Using the Arabic–English glossary
(At-home preparation; in-class activation)

Identify the roots of these words and then rewrite the list in alphabetical order in preparation for looking them up in the glossary. Check your list and correct it, if necessary, as you look up each word.

امتحان   واسع   طالب   طاولة   مبسوط

ممكن   مرحبا   مكتب   تمرين   تفضل

الوحدة العاشرة
Unit Ten

In this unit:

Two more spellings of alif: ى and ـٰ

Formal Arabic

Grammatical Endings ـِ ـَ ـُ ـِ ـَ ـُ أَ

Handwriting

Calligraphy

>> Letters and Sounds

أَلِف مَقـصورة ى

Alif maqSuura, also called أَلـف بِـصـورة الـيـاء, alif in the shape of yaaʾ, is a variant spelling of alif that can only occur at the end of a word. This shape of alif is a spelling convention that dates back to the writing of the Qur'an. It is pronounced just like the regular alif. When the long vowel alif occurs at the end of a word, it is usually spelled with alif maqSuura. However, remember that non-Arabic words and names are not spelled with alif maqSuura but with regular alif, as in آنا, أَمريكا, روسيا, and ريبيكا.

🎧 Listening Exercise 1. Listening to ى (At home)

Listen to the following examples of words ending in ى and repeat:

٣. مَشــى	٢. إلى	١. عَلــى
٦. مُثَنّــى	٥. اِنْتَهى	٤. بَكـى

🎧 Writing

ى   ــى

ى is a connector, and since it only occurs in final position, it has only the two shapes you see above. It is written exactly like final ي, except that it has no dots. In other words, final ي and ى are distinguished by the two dots of the ي, except in Egypt, where both are normally written without dots. Watch Ustaaz El-Shinnawi write this letter and copy the example:

Copy the prepositions إلى and على as shown:

عـلى إلى

Copy and read aloud the following female names that end in ى:

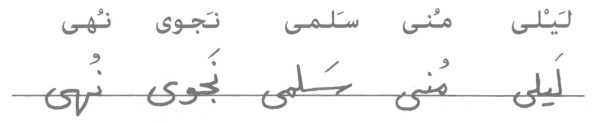

لَيْلى   مُنى   سَلمى   نَجوى   نُهى

ألف قصيرة ــٰ (or dagger alif)

This symbol, called ألف قصيرة in Arabic, is also called dagger alif because its shape resembles a small dagger. It represents an old spelling of alif from early Qur'anic writing that survives today in a handful of common words and names. It is pronounced exactly like the long vowel alif.

🎧 Listening Exercise 2. Listening to length in dagger alif

Listen to these words containing ــٰ and repeat, and give special attention to the length of this vowel:

١. هٰذا   ٢. لٰكِن   ٣. اللّٰه   ٤. عَبد الرَحمٰن

The words below are the most commonly used words that are spelled with dagger alif. Learn to recognize them, and remember that they are all pronounced with a long vowel, just as if they were spelled with alif.

١. هٰذا **this** (masc., formal)

٢. هٰذِهِ **this** (fem., formal)

٣. اللّٰه **God**

٤. ولٰكِن **but**

Writing

ا
—

This vowel most often occurs in ligatures of الله, such as ﷲ, and in fully vowelled texts. Otherwise, it is rarely written. When dagger alif is written, it is drawn as a short vertical stroke above the consonant it follows. Make sure it is precisely vertical so that it may be distinguished easily from the slanted fatHa. Copy the examples, and practice writing and pronouncing the words ولٰكن and الله :

الله

ولٰكن

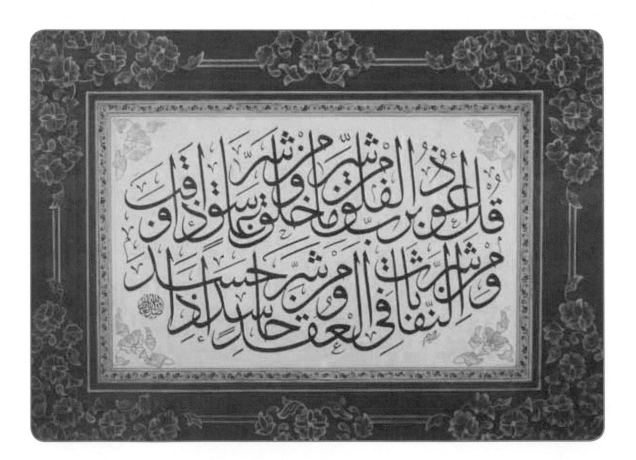

Formal Arabic

Throughout this book we have presented both formal and spoken forms of Arabic and have not been concerned about drawing sharp distinctions between these two registers of Arabic. We mentioned briefly in unit 1 that spoken Arabic, or العامّيّة , is the mode used for interaction, interpersonal relations, individual and social identity, intimacy, emotion, and connection. Formal Arabic, which we call الفُصحى , is used in presentational modes, where information or artistry is being presented in a public context. It tends to be monologue rather than dialogue, and narrative or expository in mode. It is meant to inform, impress, and enrapture rather than to express familiarity or intimacy. Together, these two registers form a single language that is nonetheless rich in variation.

By now you have an impression of the extent of overlap between the two registers. A few of the most common everyday words differ in one dialect or another, but most vocabulary and structure is shared. In professional contexts, the two registers overlap to an even greater extent. However, there is one aspect in which formal Arabic clearly departs from spoken Arabic, and this is the system of grammatical or case endings.

Grammatical Endings

In this section you will learn to recognize certain grammatical markers that are used in the highest register of formal Arabic. These markers can occur on the ends of nouns and adjectives, and some of them can occur on verbs. You will hear and see them in formal speech, poetry, sacred texts, and children's stories and schoolbooks, as you saw in unit 1.

تَنْوين

The word tanwiin, derived from the name of the letter نون , refers to the *n* sound in these three endings:

١. تَنوين فَتحة ـً (pronounced *an*)

٢. تَنوين ضَمّة ـٌ (pronounced *un*)

٣. تَنوين كَسرة ـٍ (pronounced *in*)

The *n* sound is represented in writing by the doubling of the short vowel symbol. In formal Arabic these endings occur on indefinite nouns and adjectives, and they indicate certain grammatical functions of words in a sentence. Except in very formal situations, such as public addresses, they are rarely used in speaking and are only written in vowelled texts. They are for the most part superfluous to comprehension, since speech and normal prose rely on other grammatical devices such as word order to convey meaning. For the time being you do not need to worry about their meanings; you are expected to recognize them simply as "grammatical endings" when you hear them. Remember that the ة taa marbuuTa is pronounced as ت before tanwiin, as you will hear in Listening Exercise 3.

🎧 Listening Exercise 3. Recognizing tanwiin endings

Listen to the following words being read three times, once with each tanwiin ending. Whether you hear *un*, *an*, or *in*, the meaning of each of these words remains the same: *a car, a man,* and *a woman.*

١. سيّارةٌ / سيّارةً / سيّارةٍ

٢. رجلٌ / رجلاً / رجلٍ

٣. اِمرأةٌ / اِمرأةً / اِمرأةٍ

🎧 Writing

أَ ـُ ـْ ـِ

Watch Ustaaz El-Shinnawi write these grammatical endings and copy his movements.

_____

_____

ـً

تَنـوِيــن الفَتْح

The first ending, pronounced *an*, may occur on indefinite nouns and adjectives. Of the three tanwiin endings, it is the only one you will see in unvowelled texts and the only one used in everyday speech. You have already learned several words that end in تَنـوِيـن الفَـتْح, as you will see in Listening Exercise 4.

🎧 Listening Exercise 4. Familiar words ending in تنوين الفتح

Listen to and repeat these familiar words that end in تنوين الفـتح, and note the spelling with alif:

٣. مَرحَبًا   ٢. عَفوًا   ١. شُكرًا

٥. أهلًا وسهـلًا   ٤. أهلًا

As you can see, تنـوين الفـتح has two different written forms.

ـً اً   ـً

The form on the right above, a double fatHa, is used on words that end in ة and اء (alif followed by hamza). The form on the left, in which تنوين الفـتح rests on an alif seat, is used in most other cases. Compare the spelling of the words in row A to that of the words in row B:

A. ساعةً   استاذةً   مساءً   سماءً

B. شُكراً   عَفواً   جِدّاً   أهلاً

Like other short vowel markings, the double fatHa in تنوين الفتح is not normally written in unvocalized texts. However, the alif seat that represents تنوين الفتح is always written where required, which means that alif at the end of a word usually represents تنوين الفتح rather than a long vowel. Compare the vocalized words in row B above to the same words, unvocalized this time, in row C below:

C. شكرا   عفوا   جدا   اهلا

The function of final alif as a seat for تنوين الفتح may be easily distinguished from the vowel alif since, as you have learned, Arabic words do not usually end in alif (few Arabic words end in a long vowel, and those that do end in alif are likely take the ى). Therefore, when you see an Arabic word that ends in alif, such as شكرا or أهلا, it is very likely that the alif represents تنوين الفتح. Remember also that when you hear *an* at the end of a word, it usually indicates تنوين الفتح (not to be confused with the human adjectival ending ان that you hear in words like تعبان and بردان). Practice writing تنوين الفتح by copying these familiar words:

شُكراً   عَفواً   مَرحَبًا   أهلاً وسهلاً

تَنوين الضَّمّ

This symbol is called تَنوين الضَّمّ and is pronounced *un*. It represents a certain grammatical ending on indefinite nouns and adjectives. You will see or hear it only in fully vowelled texts and formal speeches.

🎧 Listening Exercise 5. Recognizing تَنوين الضَّمّ

Listen to the following examples of تَنوين الضَّمّ and repeat:

٣. قلمٌ   ٢. استاذةٌ   ١. كتابٌ

٥. طالبٌ   ٤. ساعةٌ

Written تَنوين الضَّمّ has two main variants, both of which are commonly used and signify the same sound and meaning. You see above, on the right, two Dammas, written close together, and on the left, a Damma with a hooked tail. We will not be using تَنوين الضَّمّ for some time, but you may see or hear it, so learn to recognize these as variants of this grammatical ending. Practice writing it by copying the examples:

كتابٌ أستاذةٌ قلمٌ ساعةٌ طالبٌ

تَنوين الكَسْر

This symbol is called تَنـويـن الكَسْر and is pronounced *in*. It represents the third and final grammatical ending that can occur on indefinite nouns and adjectives. Like تَنوين الضَّمّ, it only appears in fully vocalized texts and formal contexts.

🎧 Listening Exercise 6. Recognizing تَنـويـن الكَسْر

Listen to the following examples of تنـويـن الكسـر and repeat:

٣. قلمٍ   ٢. استاذةٍ   ١. كتابٍ

٥. طالبٍ   ٤. ساعةٍ

When it is written in vowelled texts, تنـويـن الكسـر is always written the same way: two kasras. Practice writing it by copying the examples:

كتابٍ أُستاذةٍ قلمٍ ساعةٍ طالبٍ

You will learn more about the usage of تَنـويـن الضَّمّ and تَنـويـن الكَسْر when you begin to study the case system of formal Arabic. For now, we will not use them because they are not used in everyday speech, and informal Arabic does not rely on them to convey meaning. However, you will soon learn more about تَنـويـن الفـتح, which does appear in spoken Arabic in expressions such as شكراً and أهـلاً وسـهلاً.

ُ
ـ   ـَ
ـ   ـِ

Definite Endings

Definite nouns and adjectives take short vowel endings فتحة , ضمّة , and كسرة (and present tense verbs take a similar set). You hear an example of this in the expression السلامُ عليكم , in which the Damma on السلام is a grammatical ending. Like the indefinite تنوين endings, these grammatical endings are only used in formal situations and are only written in fully vowelled texts. Thus, in a formal context, الطالب might be pronounced or marked: الطالبُ or الطالبَ or الطالبِ , depending on the grammatical role of الطالب in the sentence (whether, for example, a word is the subject of the sentence, the object of a verb, the object of a preposition). However, since the grammatical role of the noun in question will be clear from other sentence clues, these endings are usually superfluous to meaning in normal prose. The important thing for you to remember is that all three of these mean *the student.*

🎧 Listening Exercise 7. Listening to grammatical endings ُ ـَ ـِ

Listen to these words and phrases read with grammatical endings فتحة , ضمة , and كسرة:

١. الطالبُ / الطالبَ / الطالبِ

٢. الأستاذةُ / الأستاذةَ / الأستاذةِ

٣. مدينةُ نيويورك / مدينةَ نيويورك / مدينةِ نيويورك

In addition to the grammatical meanings that these endings impart to texts in literary Arabic, they also add to the beauty and rhythm of oral performances in this register. Listening Exercise 8 introduces you to performances of literary and religious texts. Not only the texts but also the oral performances of them are highly valued in Arab culture.

🎧 Listening Exercise 8. Examples of Formal Arabic

Listen to the recitations of poetry, the Qur'an, and the Bible.

a. From a pre-Islamic ode by Tarafa, الموسوعة العالمية للشعر العربي www.adab.com
b. Famous Qur'an reader Shaykh Abd al-Basit reads from the Qur'an,
قراءة من سورة يوسف للشيخ عبد الباسط عبد الصمد www.mp3quran.net/basit
c. Greek Orthodox Bishop Elias Qurban recites from the Easter Mass in Tripoli,
قداس الفصح المقدس للمطران إلياس قربان متروبوليت طرابلس والكورة للروم الارثوذكس Lebanon

When children start school, they are taught to read with these endings so that they are exposed to and learn to understand the formal register of Arabic. Drill 1 will give you an idea of what this is like.

Drill 1. Reading aloud in formal Arabic (In class)

Read aloud the following phrases that are written in formal Arabic and vocalized:

١. هٰذِهِ أمرَأَةٌ ذَكِيَّةٌ فِعلاً !

٢. هٰذا رجلٌ طويلٌ جِدّاً !

٣. جامعةُ محمّدٍ الخامِس في مدينةِ الرّباطِ.

٤. المكتبةُ في مدينَتِـنا قديمةٌ ولكنّي أُحِبُّها كثيراً.

٥. أُريدُ سيّارةً جميلةً!

٦. هٰذِهِ قصّةٌ طويلة، ولَيسَ عندي وَقتٌ الآنَ .

٧. أشاهدُ فيلماً كلَّ أسبوعٍ ، في البيتِ أو في السّينما .

٨. أَسكُنُ في بيتٍ صغيرٍ في مَدينةٍ كبيرة .

٩. يذهَبُ الولدُ إلى بيتِ رَفيقِهِ ويَلعَبُ معَهُ .

>> **Writing Styles**

Handwriting

As you have been learning, Arabic handwriting differs from print in several ways, such as the joining of two dots into a bar, and the ways that the shapes ــحـ and ــمـ are connected with other letters. In addition, handwriting itself varies according to both regional and individual style. For example, the teeth of ــســ and ــشــ are normally written in North African handwriting.

The biggest variation you will find in the shape of the letters will be in the word-final shapes. In Egypt, for example, the letters ق , ض , and ـن are sometimes written without their dots and are given a hook on the end of their tails instead when they occur in word-final position. Another letter that shows word-final variation is ـة. Take a look at the below examples.

With practice, you will gradually learn to recognize various handwriting styles and conventions. Look at various styles and imitate the ones you like best as you develop your own style.

Drill 2. Reading handwriting styles
(At-home preparation; in-class activation)

Read as much as you can of the following handwriting samples. Look for familiar words and try to guess new ones from context. After reading, write a similar passage that provides information about yourself.

Sample 1:

أهلاً وسهلاً ومرحباً ،

اسمي جورج اسطفان وأنا من مدينة دمشق في سوريا. عندي ٢ إخوة وأنا استاذ في جامعة دمشق. زوجتي اسمها نيكول وهي دكتورة وعندنا بنت صغيرة وحلوة اسمها لينا.

أحبّ مدينة دمشق وإن شاء الله اشوفكم هنا قريباً.

سلاماتي إليكم   جورج

Sample 2:

أهلا وسهلا ومرحبا

اسمي نسرين الوراري وأنا من تونس من مدينة
أريانة. أدرس في كلية العلوم الإنسانية والإجتماعية
بتونس العاصمة. عندي أخ واحد وهو طالب بالسنة
الثالثة في نفس الكلية. منذ سنتين ذهبت
عائلتي لتسكن في نابل وهي مدينة جميلة
في الشمال ولكن أنا وأخي نسكن في العاصمة لأنا ندرس
ونعمل هناك.

مع السلامة

Sample 3:

السلام عليكم

أنا اسمي حاتم شريف. أنا من مدينة بورسعيد
أدرس الموسيقى في الاكاديمية الموسيقى. أخي معي
في القاهرة. هو طالب في جامعة القاهرة. أسكن
مع أخي في غرفة في بنسيون صغير في الجيزة
أذهب بالاوتوبيس إلى الاكاديمية كل صباح

Your paragraph:

_____

_____

_____

_____

_____

_____

_____

Culture: The Development of the Arabic Writing System

The Arabic writing system is believed to have evolved from the Aramaic script through the Nabateans, who were Arab tribes who lived to the north of the Arabian Peninsula (present-day Jordan) in pre-Islamic times. This early version of Arabic script survives in inscriptions that date back to the third and fourth centuries AD, which represent the earliest known of many stages of development. Although writing was known in the Arabian Peninsula before Islam, it was the early Muslims who developed the script that we know today, in order to preserve the text of the Qur'an by writing it down. Tradition holds that the first compilation of the Qur'an was recorded during the reign of عُثمان, the third Caliph (d. AD 656). Even then, however, the script was not complete, for surviving fragments show text devoid of short vowel markings and dots. The addition of short vowel signs began during the reign of Ali (علـي), the fourth Caliph (d. AD 661), and the dots that distinguish between letters of similar shape were added during Umayyad rule, around the end of the seventh century. Further development of the individual shapes of letters occurred at the beginning of the Abbasid period (from AD 750).

🎧 Calligraphy

Calligraphy is a highly developed art form. Since the time of the earliest script, called Kufic, artists have continuously developed new styles and designs. Qur'anic verses, poetry, and proverbs written in intricate scripts often adorn books, monuments, and public buildings. Professional calligraphers combine form and meaning by working Qur'anic verses into pictures wherein the letters and dots form a design. Watch Ustaaz El-Shinnawi write the words ألف باء and اللـغة الـعـربيـة in various calligraphic styles, look at other samples of Arabic calligraphy, and visit an Arabic calligrapher in his shop in Cairo.

تمربحمد اللّه

The purpose of both glossaries is to allow you to look up words you have already learned but may have forgotten. Looking up new words is not encouraged; you will learn them soon enough. Fluency is built up faster if you focus on using the words you know rather than focusing on what you would like to say right now.

In this glossary the formal or written form of a word or expression is listed in Arabic script and spoken forms are shown in transliteration. Transliteration is provided so that you can use the glossary from the outset, before knowing all the letters, and so that you can correctly pronounce the words you look up. The written version in Arabic script serves as a spelling reference. Egyptian and Syrian words are identified by the same colors that are used throughout the *Alif Baa* materials. Proper nouns are given in formal Arabic except for the name Egypt. Initial hamza is indicated in this glossary except when it is elidable.

The transliteration system used here is the same one that is presented in unit 1. We have used punctuation in the glossary to indicate certain things. Slashes separate masculine and feminine forms and alternate words (in cases where more than one word is common) are separated by a semicolon. For example:

Meaning	maSri	shaami	Formal /written
big	kibiir/a	kbiir/e	كَبير/ة

Occasionally you will see a short vowel in parentheses, which represents a vowel sound that is sometimes elided, depending on whether or not the previous word in a sentence ends in a vowel. The definite article is separated by a hyphen, following the practice of most academic transliteration systems.

English	Arabic
Algeria	الـجَزائـِر
and	وَ ,w ,wi
angry (upset or sad)	زَعـلان/ة ,zaᶜlaan/e ,zaᶜlaan/a
Arab, Arabic	عَرَبـيّ/ة ,ᶜarabi/ᶜarabiyye ,ᶜarabi/ᶜarabiyya
at, in (location in space and time)	فـي ,fi;bi ,fi
automobile, car	سَيـّارة ,sayyaara ,ᶜarabiyya
Bahrain	البَحْرَين
bathroom	حَمّام ,Hammam; twaaleet ,twaleet; Hammam
beautiful, pretty	جَميل/ة ,Hilw/e ,Hilw/a
big	كَبير/ة ,kbiir/e ,kibiir/a
black (masc.)	أَسـوَد ,aswad ,iswid
book	كِتـاب ,ktaab ,kitaab
bookstore; library	مَكـتَبة ,maktabe ,maktaba
boy	وَلَد ,walad ,walad
boyfriend	صاحِب ,SaaHib ,SaaHib
bread	خُبـز ,khibəz ,ᶜeesh
brother	أَخ ,akhkh ,akhkh
building	بِنايـة ,binaaye ,ᶜimaara
bus	أوتوبيس ,utubiis ,utubiis
but	وَلـكِن ,bass ,bass
car	سَيـّارة ,sayyaara ,ᶜarabiyya
cat	قِطّة ,bisse ,ʾuTTa
chair	كُرسـي ,kirsi ,kursi
chicken	دَجـاج ,djaaj ,firaakh
cinema, the movies	السّينَما ,is-sinama ,is-sinima
(a) city	مَدينـة ,madiine ,midiina
(the) city of...	مَدينة... ,madiinit... ,midiinit...
class, classroom	صَفّ ,Saff ,faSl
clock; watch; hour	سـاعة ,saaᶜa ,saaᶜa

close to; near	'urayyib/a min, 'ariib/e min, قَريـب/ة مِن
coffee	'ahwa, 'ahwe, قَهْوة
cold (adjective: feeling cold)	bardaan/a, bardaan/e, بَرْدان/ة
Come in, please!	itfaDDal/i, tfaDDal/i, تَفَضّل/تَفَضّلي
Come in, please! (plural)	itfaDDalu, tfaDDalu, تَفَضّلوا
correct, right	SaHH, SaHH, صَحيح
(my) dear, darling (to a female)	Habibti, Habiibti, حَبيبَتي
(my) dear, darling (to a male)	Habiibi, Habiibi, حَبيبي
desk; office	maktab, maktab, مَكْتَب
difficult, hard	Sa^cb/a, Sa^cb/e, صَعْب/ة
distant, far from	bi^ciid/a, b^ciid/e, بَعيد/ة عَن
doctor (MD, PhD)	duktuur/a, dektoor/a, دُكْتور/ة
dog	kalb, kalb, كَلْب
door	baab, baab, باب
drill, exercise	tamriin, tamriin, تَمْرين
(I) drink	ashrab, ishrab, أشرَب
(he) drinks	yishrab, yishrab, يَشرَب
(she) drinks	tishrab, tishrab, تَشرَب
(you) drink (fem.)	tishrabi, tishrabi, تَشرَبين
(you) drink (masc.)	tishrab, tishrab, تَشرَب
easy	sahl/a, sahl/e, سَهْل/ة
Egypt	maSr, maSər, مِصْر
eight	tamanya, tmaane, (٨) ثَمانِية
examination, test	imtiHaan, imtiHaan, إمتِحان
exercise, drill	tamriin, tamriin, تَمْرين
exhausted	khalSaan/a, خَلْصان/ة
far, distant from	bi^ciid/a, b^ciid/e, بَعيد/ة عَن
feel better! get well soon!	salamtak/-ik, salaamtak/-ik, سَلامتك
feel better! (reply)	allaah yisallimak/-ik, alla ysallmak/-ik, الله يسَلّمك
fine	tamaam, tamaam, بخَير
five	khamsa, khamse, (٥) خَمْسة

four	arba^ca, arb^ca, (٤) أَرْبَعة
friend	SaaHib/SaHba, rfii'/a, صاحِب/ة
from (a source or point of origin)	min, min, مِن
get well soon! feel better!	salamtak/-ik, salaamtak/-ik, سَلامتك
reply to get well soon	allaah yisallimak/-ik, alla ysallmak/-ik, الله يِسَلِّمك
girl; daughter	bint, bint, بِنْت
girlfriend	SaHba, rfii'a, صاحِبة
(I) go	aruuH, ruuH, أَذْهَب
(he) goes	yiruuH, yruuH, يَذهَب
(she) goes	tiruuH, truuH, تَذهَب
(you) go (masc.)	tiruuH, truuH, تَذهَب
(you) go (fem.)	tiruuHi, truuHi, تَذهَبين
Let's go!	yalla; yalla biina, yalla, هَيّا بِنا
God	allaah, allaah, الله
God willing, hopefully	in shaa' allaah, inshaalla, إنْ شاءَ الله
good	kuwayyis/a, mniiH/a, جَيِّد/ة
good-bye	ma^ca s-salaama, ma^ca s-salaame, مَعَ السَّلامة
reply to good-bye	allaah yisallimak/-ik, alla ysallmak/-ik; alla ma^cak, الله يسَلِّمك
good-hearted (for people); good	Tayyib/a, Tayyib/Tayybe, طَيِّب/ة
good evening!	misaa' il-kheer, masa l-kheer, مَساء الـخَير
reply to good evening	misaa' in-nuur, masa n-nuur, مَساء النّور
good morning!	SabaaH il-kheer, SabaaH il-kheer, صَباح الـخَير
reply to good morning	SabaaH in-nuur, SabaaH in-nuur, صَباح النّور
great, fine!	tamaam, tamaam, جَيِّد
green	akhDar, akhDar, أَخْضَر
happy	mabsuuT/a, mabsuuT/a, سَعيد/ة
hard, difficult	Sa^cb/a, Sa^cb/e, صَعْب/ة
have to, need to, must	laazim, laazim, لازِم
(he) has	^candu, ^cando, عِندَهُ
(she) has	^candaha, ^canda, عِندَها

(I) have	ﻋِﻨْﺪﻱ, ʿandi, **ʿandi**
(I do not) have	ﻟَﻴﺲَ ﻋِﻨﺪﻱ, maa ʿandi, ma ʿandiish
(you) have (fem.)	ﻋِﻨﺪَﻙِ, ʿandik, **ʿandik**
(you) have (masc.)	ﻋِﻨﺪَﻙَ, ʿandak, **ʿandak**
he	ﻫُﻮَ, huwwe, huwwa
hello, hi	ﺃَﻫْﻼً ﻭﺳَﻬْﻼً, **marHaba** , ahlan; ahlan wa sahlan
hello (reply to ahlan wa sahlan)	ﺃَﻫﻼً ﺑِﻚَ / ﻟـﻚِ, **ahlan fiik/-ki**, ahlan biik/-ki
hello (Islamic)	ﺍﻟﺴَّﻼﻡ ﻋَـﻠَـﻴْـﻜُـﻢ, **as-salaamu ʿalaykum**, as-salaamu ʿalaykum
(reply to) as-salaamu ʿalaykum	ﻭﻋَـﻠَﻴْـﻜُـﻢُ ﺍﻟﺴَّـﻼﻡ, **wa ʿalaykumu s-salaam**, wa ʿalaykumu s-salaam
hello (Levantine)	ﻣَﺮﺣَـﺒـﺎً, **marHaba**
hers (possessive suffix)	ـ ﻫﺎ, **–a**, –ha
his (possessive suffix)	ـ ﻪُ, **–o**, –u
homework	ﻭﺍﺟِـﺐ, **waZiife**, waagib
hot (feeling hot)	ﺣَـﺮَّﺍﻥ/ﺓ, **mshawwib/mshawwbe**, Harraan/a
hour; clock; watch	ﺳـﺎﻋﺔ, **saaʿa**, saaʿa
house	ﺑَـﻴْﺖ, **beet**, beet
How?	ﻛَـﻴْـﻒَ؟, **kiif?**, izzayy?
How are you?	ﻛَﻴْـﻒَ ﺍﻟـﺤـﺎﻝ؟ , **kiifak/-ik?**, izzayyak/-ik?
hungry	ﺟَـﻮﻋﺎﻥ/ﺓ, **juuʿaan/e**, gaʿaan/a
I	ﺃﻧـﺎ, **ana**, ana
ill, sick	ﻣَـﺮﻳﺾ/ﺓ, **mariiD/a**, ʿayyaan/a
in (location in space and time), at	ﻓـﻲ, **bi**, fi
in the name of God	ﺑِـﺴـْﻢ ﺍﻟﻠﻪ, **bismilla**, bismilla
Iran	ﺇﻳﺮﺍﻥ
Iraq	ﺍﻟـﻌِـﺮﺍﻕ
Israel	ﺇﺳـﺮﺍﺋﻴـﻞ
it (fem.)	ﻫِـﻲَ, **hiyye**, hiyya
it (masc.)	ﻫُـﻮَ, **huwwe**, huwwa
Jordan	ﺍﻟﺄُﺭُﺩﻥ

juice	^caSiir, **^caSiir**, عَصير
kind (person)	Tayyib/a, **Tayyib/Tayybe**, طَيِّب/ة
Kuwait	الكُوَيت
large	kibiir/a, **kbiir/e**, كَبير/ة
Lebanon	لُبنان
lesson	dars, **dars**, دَرْس
library; bookstore	maktaba, **maktabe**, مَكْتَبة
Libya	ليبيا
like: see love	
little, small	Sughayyar/a, **zghiir/e**, صَغير/ة
(a) little, a little bit	shuwayya, **shwayy**, قَليلاً
long, tall	Tawiil/a, **Tawiil/e**, طَويل/ة
(I) love, like	baHibb, **bHibb**, أُحِبّ
(you) love, like (masc.)	bitHibb, **bitHibb**, تُحِبّ
(you) love, like (fem.)	bitHibbi, **bitHibbi**, تُحِبّين
(he) loves, likes	biyHibb, **biHibb**, يُحِبّ
(she) loves, likes	bitHibb, **bitHibb**, تُحِبّ
man	raagil, **rijjaal**, رَجُل
Mauritania	موريتانيا
May I be excused? (taking leave)	^can iznak/–ik, **^can iznak/–ik**, عَن إذنِك
(it/that) means; that is	ya^cni, **ya^cni**, يَعني
milk	laban, **Haliib**, حَليب
Miss	aanisa, **aanse**, آنِسة
(a) mistake, wrong	ghalaT, **ghalaT**, غَلَط
Mr.	sayyid, **sayyid**, سَيِّد
Mrs.	sayyida, **sayyde**, سَيِّدة
money	filuus, **maSaari**, مال
Morocco	المَغرِب
movie	film, **film**, فيلم
the movies, the cinema	is-sinima, **is-sinama**, السّينَما
must, need to, have to (fixed form)	laazim, **laazim**, لازِم

my (possessive suffix)	‑i, **‑i**, ‑ـي
name	ism, **ism**, اِسـم
(my) name is	ismi, **ismi**, اِسمي
near; close to	ʾurayyib/a min, **ʾariib/e min**, قَـريـب/ة مِن
need to, must, have to (fixed form)	laazim, **laazim**, لازِم
neighbor	gaar/a, **jaar/a**, جـار/ة
never mind, it's OK	maᶜlishsh, **maᶜleesh**, مَعلِهش؛ مَعليش
new	gidiid/a, **jdiid/e**, جَديد/ة
news (fem.)	akhbaar, **akhbaar**, أخبار
nice, pleasant (of people)	laTiif/a, **laTiif/e**, لَطيف/ة
Nice to meet you!	itsharrafna, **tsharrafna**, تَشَرَّفنا
nine	tisᶜa, **tisᶜa**, (٩) تِسـعة
no	la, **laʾ; laa** لا
(is) not	mish, **muu**, لَيسَ
nothing	wala Haaga, **wala shi**, لا شَـيء
number	nimra, **nimra**, رَقَـم
office; desk	maktab, **maktab**, مَكتَب
OK then, fine	Tayyib; maashi, **Tayyib; maashi**, طَيِّب
old (of people)	kibiir/a, **kbiir/e**, كَبير/ة
old (of things, not people); ancient	ʾadiim/a, **ʾadiim/e**, قَـديـم/ة
Oman	عُـمـان
one	waaHid, **waaHid**, (١) واحِـد
or	walla, **walla**, أو
page	SafHa, **SafHa**, صَفحَة
Palestine	فِلَسطيـن
paper (piece of)	waraʾa, **warʾa**, وَرَقَـة
pen, pencil	ʾalam, **ʾalam**, قَـلَم
please	min faDlak/‑ik, **min faDlak/‑ik** مِن فَضلِك
please (come in; go ahead; sit down)	itfaDDal/i, **tfaDDal/i**, تَفَضّل/ تفضّلي
pleased to meet you!	itsharrafna, **tsharrafna**, تَشَرَّفنا
possible	mumkin, **mumkin**, مُـمكِن

pretty, beautiful	جَميل/ة ,Hilw/a, **Hilw/e**
problem	مُشكِلة ,mushkila, **mishkle**
professor	أُستاذ/ة ,ustaaz/a, **istaaz/e**
Qatar	قَـطَـر
question	سـُؤال ,su'aal, **su'aal**
the Qur'an	الـقُـرآن
ready	جاهِز/ة ,gaahiz/gahza, **jaahiz/jaahze**
right, correct	صَحيح ,SaHH, **SaHH**
room	غُـرْفـة ,ooDa, **ghurfe**; uuDa
sad (angry or upset)	زَعْـلان/ة ,zaᶜlaan/a, **zaᶜlaan/e**
Saudi Arabia	الـسَّـعوديّـة
(I) see; watch	أُشاهِد ,ashuuf, **shuuf**
(he) sees; watches	يُشاهِد ,yishuuf, **yshuuf**
(she) sees; watches	تُشاهِد ,tishuuf, **tshuuf**
(you) see; watch (fem.)	تُشاهِدين ,tishuufi, **tshuufi**
(you) see; watch (masc.)	تُشاهِد ,tishuuf, **tshuuf**
sentence	جُملة ,gumla, **jumle**
seven	سَـبُـعة (٧), sabᶜa, **sabᶜa**
she	هِـيَ ,hiyya, **hiyye**
short	قَـصير/ة ,'uSayyar/a, **'aSiir/e** √
sick, ill	مَريض/ة ,ᶜayyaan/a, **mariiD/a**
sister	أخْـت ,ukht, **ukht**
six	سِـتـة (٦), sitta, **sitte**
small, little	صَـغير/ة ,Sughayyar/a, **zghiir/e**
something	شَـيء ,Haaga, **shi**
something else	شَـيء آخَـر ,Haaga taani, **shi taani**
sorry! (adjective)	آسِـف/ة ,aasif/asfa, **mit'assif/mit'assfe**
spacious, wide	واسِـع/ة ,waasiᶜ/wasᶜa, **waasiᶜ/waasᶜa**
story	قِـصّة ,qiSSa, **'uSSa** \
strange, odd	غَـريب/ة ,ghariib/a, **ghariib/e**
street	شـارِع ,shaariᶜ, **shaariᶜ**

234

student	طَالِب/ة، Taalib/a, Taalib/Taalbe
Sudan	السّودان
sugar	سُكّر، sukkar, sikkar
sugar, medium	سُكّر وَسَط، maZbuuT, sikkar wasaT
Syria	سوريا
table	طاوِلة، TarabeeZa, Taawle
tall, long	طَويل/ة، Tawiil/a, Tawiil/e
tasty, good (food)	طَيِّب/ة، Tayyib/a, Tayyib/Tayybe
tea	شاي، shaay, shaay
teacher	أُستاذ/ة، ustaaz/a, istaaz/e
telephone	تِليفون، tilifoon, talifoon
telephone number	رَقِم تِليفون، nimrit tilifuun, nimrit talifuun
ten	عَشَرة (١٠)، ᶜashara, ᶜashra
test, examination	اِمْتِحان، imtiHaan, imtiHaan
thank God	الـحَمْدُ لله، il-Hamdu li-llaah, il-Hamdilla
thank you	شُكراً، shukran, shukran
that's all, only	فَقَط، bass, bass
there is	هُناك، fii, fii
there isn't	لَيسَ هُناك، ma fiish, maa fii
thirsty	عَطْشان/ة، ᶜaTshaan/a, ᶜaTshaan/e
this (fem.)	هـــذِه، di, haadi; haydi
this (masc.)	هـــذا، da, haada; hayda
three	ثَلاثة (٣)، talaata, tlaate
tired	تَعْبان/ة، taᶜbaan/a, taᶜbaan/e
tree	شَجَرة، shagara, shajra
Tunisia	تـونِس
two	اِثنـان/ اِثنَيْـن (٢)، itneen, tneen
United Arab Emirates	الإمـارات
(a) university	جامِعة، gamᶜa, jaamᶜa
(the) university (of)	جامِعة...، gamᶜit ..., jaamᶜit ...
upset (angry or sad)	زَعلان/ة، zaᶜlaan/a, zaᶜlaan/e

veil, head covering	Higaab, Hjaab, حِجاب
(I) want	ana ᶜaayiz/ᶜayza, **biddi**, أُريد
(he) wants	huwwa ᶜaayiz, **biddo**, يُريد
(she) wants	hiyya ᶜayza, **bidda**, تُريد
(you) want (fem.)	inti ᶜayza, **biddik**, تُريدين
(you) want (masc.)	inta ᶜaayiz, **biddak**, تُريد
(I) watch; see	ashuuf, **ashuuf**, أُشاهِد
(he) watches; sees	yishuuf, **yshuuf**, يُشاهِد
(she) watches; sees	tishuuf, **tshuuf**, تُشاهِد
(you) watch; see (fem.)	tishuufi, **tshuufi**, تُشاهِدين
(you) watch (masc.)	tishuuf, **tshuuf**, تُشاهِد
watch; clock; hour	saaᶜa, **saaᶜa**, ساعـة
water	mayya, **mayy**, مـاء
weird, strange	ghariib/a, **ghariib/e**, غـَريب/ة
welcome	ahlan wa sahlan, **ahlan wa sahlan**, أهْلاً وسَـهْلاً
welcome (formal)	مَرحَباً بـِ
reply to welcome	ahlan wa sahlan biik/-ki, **ahla(n) fiik/-ki**, أهْلاً وسَـهْلاً بك
you're welcome!	il-ᶜafw, **ahla w sahla fiik/-ki**, عَـفواً
well, fine (response to How are you?)	kuwayyis, **mniiH**, بخَير
What?	ee?, **shuu?**, ما؟
What's wrong (with you)?	maalak/-ik?, **shubak?/-ik?**, ما بـِكَ/بِكِ؟ما لَك/ما لَكِ؟
Where?	feen?, **ween?**, أيْنَ؟
Where (are you) from?	(inta) mineen?, **(inte) min ween?**, مِن أيْنَ (أنت)؟
white (masc.)	abyaD, **abyaD**, أبْيَض
wide, spacious	waasiᶜ/wasᶜa, **waasiᶜ/waasᶜa**, واسِـع/ة
window	shubbaak, **shibbaak**, شُـبّاك
with (people)	maᶜa, **maᶜ**, مَـعَ
with (things; instrumental)	bi-, **bi-**, بـِ -
woman	sitt, **mara**, امـرأة
word	kilma, **kilme**, كَـلِمـة

wrong, a mistake	ghalaT, ghalaT, غَـلَط
Yemen	الْـيَمـَن
yes	aywa, ee, نَعَم
you (fem.)	inti, inti, أَنْتِ
you (masc.)	inta, inte, أَنْتَ
you (fem., polite)	HaDritik, HaDərtik, حَضْرَتُكِ
you (masc., polite)	HaDritak, HaDərtak, حَضْرَتُكَ
young, small	Sughayyar/a, zghiir/e, صَغير/ة
young people, "guys"	shabaab, shabaab, شباب
your (fem. suffix)	–ik, –ik, كِ -
your (masc. suffix)	–ak, –ak, كَ -
zero	ziiru; Sifr, Sifər, صِفُر (٠)

قـاموس عربي – إنجليزي
Arabic–English Glossary

The purpose of this glossary is to allow you to look up words you have learned but whose meaning you may have forgotten. We have included the main forms of all active vocabulary in the book, including colloquial forms that are used in writing. Words are listed in alphabetical order by their consonant root according to Arabic practice rather than according to spelling. If you cannot find a word by looking for it alphabetically, try to identify its root or core consonants, and look it up under those letters.

In this glossary both formal and spoken forms are listed in Arabic script and transliterations are not given. **Please do not use this glossary for pronunciation.** If you want to know the spoken forms, look up the word in the English–Arabic glossary. Neither the regular colloquial pronunciation shifts that you learn in *Alif Baa*, such as hamza for qaaf and the Levantine pronunciation of final fatHa as *e*, are marked, nor are the final short vowels of masculine and feminine possessive endings كَ and كِ (formal كَ and كِ), as these are introduced in unit 2. Most entries in this glossary are written in the blue color that identifies the formal/written form, which indicates that they represent standard or shared forms. When an Egyptian (green) or Levantine (purple) form of the same word differs, they are shown in that color. When one or both dialects have a different word, this is listed as a separate entry. Slashes separate masculine and feminine forms, with the masculine form listed first.

Meaning	maSri (Egyptian)	shaami (Levantine)	Formal /written
Man	راجِل	رِجّال	رَجُل

English	Arabic
brother	أخ
sister	أُخت
may I be excused? (taking leave)	إذْن: عَن إِذْنك
Jordan	الأُردُن
professor, teacher	أُستاذ/ة
How?	ازّيّ؟
How are you?	ازّيّـك؟
Israel	إسـرائيل
sorry! (adjective)	آسِف/ة، مِتأَسِّف/ة
sir/madam	أَفنِدِم
God	الله
(reply to) maᶜa ssalaama and salaamtak	الله يسَـلِّـمَك
God willing	إنْ شاءَ الله
in the name of God	بِسـم الله
a response to 'How are you?'; thank God	الحَمدُ لله
there is no god but God	لا إله إلا الله
wow! (expression of admiration)	ما شاءَ الله
United Arab Emirates	الإمـارات
I	أنا
you (fem.)	أنتِ، إنتِ، إنتِ
you (masc.)	أنتَ، إنتَ، إنتَ
Miss	آنِسـة
hello, welcome; Syrian only: you're welcome	أَهْلاً وسَـهْلاً
(reply to hello), welcome; thank you,	أَهْلاً وسَـهْلاً بك، أَهلا فيك، أَهْلاً بِيك
or	أو
bus	أوتوبيس
room	أوضة
yes	إيه، أيَوَه
Iran	إيران

Where?	أَيْنَ؟
What?	إيه؟
with (things; instrumental); (Syrian only: in)	بِـ
well, fine (formal response to "kayf al-Haal?")	بِخَير
I want	بِدّي
you want	بِدَّك / بِدِّك
he wants	بِدّه (بِدّو)
she wants	بِدّها
cold (adjective: feeling cold)	بَرْدان/ة
only; that's all	بَسّ، بَسّ
cat	بِسّة
far from, distant	بَعيد/ة عَن
girl; daughter	بِنْت
building	بِنايـة
door	باب
house, home	بَيْت
white	أَبْيَض
nine	تِسْعة (٩)
tired	تَعْبان/ة
telephone	تِليفون
great, fine	تَمام، تَمام
toilet; bathroom	تواليت، تواليت
Tunisia	تـونِس
three	ثَلاثة (٣)، تلاتة، تلاتة
eight	ثَمانِية (٨)، تَمانة، تَمانية
two	اِثـنان، اِثـنَيْن (٢)، اِتنـين، اِتنـين
new	جَديد/ة
Algeria	الـجَزائِر
university	جامِعة
sentence	جُملة
beautiful, pretty	جَميل/ة

ready	جاهِز/ة
neighbor	جار/ة
hungry	جَوْعان/ة، جوعان/ة، جَعان/ة
good	جَيِّد/ة
(I) love, like	أُحِبّ، بحِبّ، باحِبّ
(you) love, like (masc.)	تُحِبّ، بِتحِبّ، بِتحِبّ
(you) love, like (fem.)	تُحِبِّين، بِتحِبِّي، بِتحِبِّي
(he) loves, likes	يُحِبّ، بيحِبّ، بيحِبّ
(she) loves, likes	تُحِبّ، بِتحِبّ، بِتحِبّ
(my) darling, dear (to a female)	حَبيبَتي
(my) darling, dear (to a male)	حَبيبي
veil, head covering	حِجاب
hot (feeling hot)	حَرّان/ة
you (fem., polite)	حَضْرَتُكِ، حَضِرتك، حَضْرتك
you (masc., polite)	حَضْرَتُكَ، حَضِرتك، حَضْرتك
milk	حَليب
pretty, beautiful	حِلو/ة، حِلو/ة
response to How are you?; thank God	الْحَمْدُ لله
bathroom, toilet	حَمّام
thing, something, anything	حاجة
something else, anything else	حاجة تاني
news (fem.)	أَخْبار
bread	خُبْز، خِبْز
pita bread	خُبْز عَرَبي، خِبْز عَرَبي
green	أَخْضَر
exhausted	خَلْصان/ة
five	خَمْسة (٥)
this (masc.)	دا
chicken	دَجاج، دُجاج
lesson	دَرْس
doctor (MD, PhD)	دُكْتور/ة

this (fem.)		دي
I go		أَذْهَب
you go (masc.)		تَذهَب
you go (fem.)		تَذهَبِين
he goes		يَذهَب
she goes		تَذهَب
four		أَرْبَعة (٤)
man		رَجُل، رِجّال، راجِل
hello		مَرحَبًا، مَرحَبا
friend		رفيق/ة
number		رَقَم
telephone number		رَقَم تِليفون
I go		أَروح، أَروح
you (masc.) go; she goes		تِروح، تِروح
you (fem.) go		تُروحي، تِروحي
he goes		يُروح، يِروح
I want		أُريد
you (masc.) want; she wants		تُريد
you (fem.) want		تُريدين
he wants		يُريد
upset (angry or sad)		زَعْلان/ة
zero		زيرو
question		سُؤال
seven		سَبْعة (٧)
woman, lady		سِتّ، سِتّ
six		سِتّة (٦)
happy		سَعيد/ة
Saudi Arabia		السَّعوديّة
sugar		سُكَّر، سِكَّر
sugar, medium		سُكَّر وَسَط، سِكَّر وَسَط
hello, Greetings! (Islamic greeting)		السَّلامُ عَلَيكُم

Feel better! Get well soon!	سَلامتَك! سَلامتَك!
name	اِسـم
(my) name is	اِسمي
easy	سَهْل/ة
black (masc.)	أَسـوَد، إسـود
Sudan	السّـودان
Mr., sir	سَيِّد
Mrs., lady	سَيِّدة، سِتّ، سِتّ
Syria	سـوريّا
clock, watch, hour	سـاعة
car, automobile	سَيّارة
the movies, the cinema	السّـيـنَما
tea	شـاي
young people, "guys" (including mixed gender)	شَباب
window	شُبّاك، شِبّاك
tree	شَجَرة
I drink	أشـرَب، إِشرَب، أَشرَب
you drink (masc.)	تَشرَب، تِشرَب، تِشرَب
you drink (fem.)	تَشرَبين، تِشرَبي، تِشرَبي
he drinks	يَشرَب، يِشرَب، يِشرَب
she drinks	تَشرَب، تِشرَب، تِشرَب
street	شـارع
Nice to meet you!	تَشَرَّفنا، تُشَرَّفنا، اتْشَرَّفنا
thank you	شُكـراً
problem	مُشكِلة، مِشكـلة
I watch	أشـاهِد
you (masc.) watch; she watches	تُشـاهِد
you (fem.) watch	تُشـاهِدين
he watches	يُشـاهِد
What?	شو؟
What's wrong (with you)?	شوبَك؟ شوبِك؟

hot	مشَوِّب/ة
I see, watch	اَشوف، اَشوف
you (masc.) see, watch; she sees, watches	تشوف، تِشوف
you (fem.) see, watch	تشوفي، تِشوفي
he sees, watches	يشوف، يِشوف
something	شيء، شي
something else	شيء آخَر، شي تاني
(a) little, a little bit	شُوَيّ، شوَيّة
morning	صَباح
good morning	صَباح الخَير
response to good morning	صَباح النّور
friend (also, boyfriend/girlfriend)	صاحِب/ة
correct; Right! Correct!	صَحيح، صَحّ، صَحّ
class, classroom	صَفّ
page	صَفْحة
zero	صِفُر (٠)
difficult, hard	صَعْب/ة
small, little; young	صَغير/ة، صُغَيِّر/ة
table	طاولة، طَرابيزة
student	طالِب/ة
tall, long	طَويل/ة
good-hearted (for people); good, (for food)	طَيِّب/ة
OK then, fine	طَيِّب!
Arab, Arabic	عَرَبيّ/ة
car	عَرَبيّة
Iraq	العِراق
ten	عَشَرة (١٠)
juice	عَصير
thirsty	عَطْشان/ة
you're welcome	عَفواً، العَفو
building	عِمارة

Oman	عُمـان
May I be excused? (taking leave)	عَن إذنك
you have (masc.)	عِندَكَ، عَندَك، عَندَك
you have (fem.)	عِندَكِ، عَندِك، عَندِك
(he) has	عِندَهُ، عَندهُ، عَندُه
(she) has	عِندَها، عَندها، عَندَها
I have	عِنـدي، عَندي، عَندي
I do not have	لَيسَ عِندي، ما عَندي، ما عَنديش
(it/that) means; that is	يَعني
want (adjective)	عايِز/ة
bread	عيش
sick, ill	عَيّان/ة
strange, odd	غَـريب/ة
Morocco	المَغرِب
room	غُـرْفـة
wrong, a mistake	غَـلَـط
chicken	فِراخ
class, classroom	فَصل
please	مِـن فَضْلِكَ
please (come in; go ahead; sit down)	تَفَضَّل/تَفَضَّلي، تُفَضَّل/تفَضَّلي، اِتْفَضَّل/اتفَضَّلي
please (come in; go ahead; sit down) (plural)	تَفَضَّلوا، تُفَضَّلوا، اِتفَضَّلوا
that's all, only	فَقَط
movie	فيلم
money	فِلوس
Palestine	فِلَسْطيـن
in (location in time or space)	فـي
Where?	فين؟
there is	فيه، فيه
old (of things, not people); ancient	قَـديم/ة
the Qur'an	الـقُرآن
close to; near	قَـريـب/ة مِن، قُـرَيّب من

Story	قِصّة
cat	قِطّة، قُطّة
Qatar	قَطَر
short	قَصير/ة، قُصَيَّر/ة
(a) little, a little bit	قَليلاً
pen, pencil	قَلَم
coffee	قَهْوة
American coffee	قَهْوة أَمْريكيّة
Arabic coffee	قَهْوة عَرَبيّة
your (fem. suffix)	ـكِ، ـكِ، كِ
your (masc. suffix)	ـكَ، ـكَ، كَ
large, big; old (of people)	كَبير/ة
book	كِتاب
office; desk	مَكْتَب
library; bookstore	مَكْتَبة
chair	كُرسي
dog	كَلب
word	كَلِمة، كِلِمة، كِلَمَة
Kuwait	الكُوَيت
good, fine	كوِيّس/ة
How?	كَيْفَ؟، كيف؟
How are you?	كَيْفَ الحال؟، كيفك؟
no	لا
nothing	لا شَيْء، وَلا شي
milk	لَبن
Lebanon	لُبنان
must, need to, have to (fixed form)	لازِم، لازِم
nice, pleasant (of people)	لَطيف/ة
but	وَلٰكِن
Libya	ليبيا
(is) not	لَيسَ

there isn't	لَيسَ هُناك
What?	ما؟
What's wrong?	ما بِك؟، ما لَك؟/ ما لِك
OK	ماشِي، ماشِي
I do not have	لَيسَ عِندي، ما عَندي، ما عَنديش
there isn't	ما فيه، ما فيش
happy	مَبسوط/ة، مَبسوط/ة
test, examination	اِمْتِحان
city	مَدينة
woman	اِمْرأة، مَرة
sick, ill	مَريض/ة
drill, exercise	تَمرين
evening	مَساء
good evening	مَساء الخَير
response to good evening	مَساء النّور
(am/are/is) not	مِش
Egypt	مِصر، مَصر
money	مَصاري
(coffee with) medium or "just right" sugar	مَضبوط
with (people)	مَعَ
good-bye	مَعَ السّلامة
never mind, that,s OK	معليش، مَعلِهش
(it is) possible, can	مُمكِن
from (a source or point of origin)	مِن
from where?	مِن أَيْنَ؟، مِن وين؟، مِنين؟
good, fine	منيح/ة
(am/are/is) not	مو
Mauritania	موريتانيا
money	مال
water	ماء، مَيّ، مَيّة
yes	نَعم

number	نِمرة، نِمرة
telephone number	نِمرة تليفون، نِمرة تليفون
wrong number!	النِمرة غَـلَـط، النِمرة غَـلَـط
this (fem.)	هـــلِذِه، هادي؛ هَيدي
this (masc.)	هـــلذا، هادا؛ هَيدا
there is	هُناك
he, it (masc.)	هُوَ، هُوِّ، هُوَّ
she, it (fem.)	هِيَ، هِيِّ، هِيَّ
his (possessive suffix)	ـــهُ، ـُه، ـُه
hers (possessive suffix)	ـــها
and	وَ
homework	واجِب
one	واحِد (١)
piece of paper	وَرَقة، وَرقة
wide, spacious	واسِع/ة
homework	وَظيفة
or	وَلاّ، وَلاّ
nothing	وَلا حاجة، وَلا شـي
boy	وَلَد
but	وَلـٰكِـن
Where?	وين؟
my (possessive suffix)	ـــي
signal that you are addressing someone directly	يا
Let's go!	يَلا، يلا بينا
Yemen	الْيَمَـن

Credits

The photographs and handwriting samples were provided by the authors.

(P. 4)

Tarafa, "There are ruins of Khawla at Barwata Tahmidi" (The Hanging Ode) or Mu'allaqa of Imru'u l-Qays. Available at www.adab.com/modules.php?name=Sh3er& doWhat=shqas&qid=14324&r=&rc=0

(P. 5)

Qur'an 110;

سورة النصر من القرآن الكريم

(P. 5)

Reprinted with permission from the Arabic Bible Outreach Ministry. The Bible, 1–5 Genesis (Van Dyke Arabic Bible translation) available at www.arabicbible.com/bible/ doc_bible.htm

الخدمة العربية للكرازة بالإنجيل

(P. 6)

Reprinted with permission. *Arabic Language Textbook for Second Grade Elementary, First Semester,* (Qatar Ministry of Education, 2008), p. 24.

اللغة العربية للصف الثاني الابتدائي، الفصل الدراسي الأول، وزارة التعليم بقطر 2008

(P. 6)

"693,000 Lose Their Jobs in the US," *Al-Hayat* [newspaper], January 8, 2009.

من جريدة الحياة 8/1/2009

(P. 182)

Advertisement from *Al-Arab* [newspaper], December 28, 2008.

جريدة العرب 28/12/2008

(P. 193)

Right column, from top: *Al-Ahram* newspaper, Egypt; *Al-Quds al-Arabi* newspaper, UK; *al-Ittihad* newspaper, United Arab Emirates.
Left column, from top: *Al-Jazirah* newspaper, Saudi Arabia; *al-Qabas* newspaper, Kuwait; Bahrain, *al-Watan* newspaper; *al-Hayat* newspaper, Lebanon.

(P. 199)

Used by permission. Mahmoud Qasim and Seif Salmawy, eds., *Egyptian Cinema Posters* (Cairo: Dar al-Shuruq, 2005), 84-88.

أفيش السينما المصرية، إعداد محمود قاسم وسيف سلماوي (القاهرة: دار الشروق، 2005 ص) 84-88

(P. 203)

Arabic translation of "College and University Education in the United States" in eJournal USA, vol. 10, no. 1 (Nov. 2005).

(P. 214)

Muhammad al-Mindi, *A Prayer: Supplications from the writings of Sayed Ibrahim* (Cairo: Nubar Printing House, n.d.).

محمد المندي، دعاء: أدعية من كتابات سيد ابراهيم
(القاهرة: دار نوبار للطباعة، د. ت).

Audio, Unit 10, Listening Ex. 8a (P. 222)

Audio recording of the poem "There are ruins of Khawla at Barwata Tahmidi" (The Hanging Ode) by Tarafa is used by permission of Adab (Adab.com) and available at www.adab.com/modules.php?name=Sh3er&file=media&doWhat=lsq&shid=257&start=0

Audio, Unit 10, Listening Ex. 8b (P. 222)

Audio recording of Qur'an recitation by Shaykh Abd al-Basit used by permission of the website www.abdalbasit.com and can be found at www.mp3quran.net/.

Audio, Unit 10, Listening Ex. 8c (P. 222)

Audio recording of the Greek Orthodox Archbishop of Tripoli, Metropolitan Elias Qurban, is used by permission.

GEORGETOWN UNIVERSITY PRESS *AL-KITAAB* ARABIC LANGUAGE PROGRAM

Alif Baa: Introduction to Arabic Letters and Sounds

Alif Baa, Third Edition

Alif Baa, Student's Edition
ISBN 978-1-58901-632-3, paperback + DVD
ISBN 978-1-62616-122-1, paperback + DVD + website access card
ISBN 978-1-58901-644-6, hardcover + DVD
ISBN 978-1-62616-127-6, hardcover + DVD + website access card
* *DVD includes audio and video files; no interactive exercises*
** *Website Access Card provides 18 months of access to companion website*

Alif Baa, Teacher's Edition
ISBN 978-1-58901-705-4, paperback + DVD + answer key + website access code

Answer Key to Alif Baa, Third Edition
ISBN 978-1-58901-634-7, paperback
* *The Answer Key is included in teacher edition; it must be purchased separately if not using website*

Replacement DVD for Alif Baa, Third Edition
ISBN 978-1-58901-633-0, DVD

Companion Website Access Key for Alif Baa, Third Edition
ISBN 978-1-62616-062-0, 18 months access
* *Access to website can also be purchased directly from the **alkitaabtextbook.com** website*

Alif Baa, Second Edition

Alif Baa with Multimedia, Second Edition
ISBN 978-1-58901-506-7, paperback + DVD

Answer Key to Alif Baa, Second Edition
ISBN 978-1-58901-036-9, paperback

Replacement DVD for Alif Baa with Multimedia, Second Edition
ISBN: 978-1-58901-508-1, DVD

Al-Kitaab fii Ta^c allum al-^c Arabiyya: A Textbook for Beginning Arabic, Part One

Al-Kitaab, Part One, Third Edition

Al-Kitaab, Part One, Student's Edition
ISBN 978-1-58901-736-8, paperback + DVD
ISBN 978-1-62616-124-5, paperback + DVD + website access card
ISBN 978-1-58901-737-5, hardcover + DVD
ISBN 978-1-62616-128-3, hardcover + DVD + website access card
* *DVD includes audio and video files; no interactive exercises*
** *Website Access Card provides 18 months of access to companion website*

Al-Kitaab, Part One, Teacher's Edition
ISBN 978-1-58901-747-4, paperback + DVD + answer key + website access code

Answer Key to Al-Kitaab, Part One, Third Edition
ISBN 978-1-58901-738-2, paperback
* *The Answer Key is included in teacher edition; it must be purchased separately if not using website*

Replacement DVD for *Al-Kitaab, Part One,* Third Edition
ISBN 978-1-58901-746-7, DVD

Companion Website Access Key for *Al-Kitaab, Part One,* Third Edition
ISBN 978-1-62616-063-7, 18 months access
** Access to website can also be purchased directly from the **alkitaabtextbook.com** website*

Haki bil-Libnani: Lebanese Arabic Online Textbook and Companion Website to Al-Kitaab Part One, Third Edition

***Al-Kitaab, Part One,* with *Haki bil-Libnani* Website Access Card**
ISBN: 978-1-62616-147-4, paperback + DVD + website access card

Website Access Key for *Haki bil-Libnani: Lebanese Arabic Online Textbook and Companion Website to Al-Kitaab Part One, Third Edition*
ISBN 978-1-62616-154-2, 18 months access
** Access to website can also be purchased directly from the **alkitaabtextbook.com** website*

Al-Kitaab, Part One, Second Edition

***Al-Kitaab, Part One,* Second Edition**
ISBN 978-1-58901-104-5, paperback + DVD

Answer Key to *Al-Kitaab, Part One,* Second Edition
ISBN 978-1-58901-037-6, paperback

Replacement DVD for *Al-Kitaab, Part One,* Second Edition
ISBN: 978-1-62616-099-6, DVD

Al-Kitaab fii Ta^{c}allum al-^{c}Arabiyya: A Textbook for Intermediate Arabic, Part Two

Al-Kitaab, Part Two, Third Edition

***Al-Kitaab, Part Two,* Student's Edition**
ISBN 978-1-58901-962-1, paperback + DVD
ISBN 978-1-62616-123-8, paperback + DVD + website access card
* DVD includes audio and video files; no interactive exercises
** Website Access Card provides 18 months of access to companion website

***Al-Kitaab, Part Two,* Teacher's Edition**
ISBN 978-1-58901-966-9, paperback + DVD + answer key + website access code

Answer Key to *Al-Kitaab, Part Two,* Third Edition
ISBN 978-1-58901-965-2, paperback
* The Answer Key is included in teacher edition; it must be purchased separately if not using website

Replacement DVD for *Al-Kitaab, Part Two,* Third Edition
ISBN 978-1-58901-964-5, DVD

Companion Website Access Key for *Al-Kitaab, Part Two, Third Edition*
ISBN 978-1-62616-064-4, 18 months access
** Access to website can also be purchased directly from the **alkitaabtextbook.com** website*

<u>*Al-Kitaab, Part Two, Second Edition*</u>

    ***Al-Kitaab, Part Two*, Second Edition**
    ISBN 978-1-58901-096-3, paperback + DVD

    Answer Key to *Al-Kitaab, Part Two*, Second Edition
    ISBN 978-1-58901-097-0, paperback

    Replacement DVD for *Al-Kitaab, Part Two*, Second Edition
    ISBN: 978-1-62616-155-9, DVD

Al-Kitaab fii Ta^{c}allum al-^{c}Arabiyya: A Textbook for Intermediate Arabic, Part Three

    Al-Kitaab, Part Three
    ISBN 978-1-58901-149-6, paperback + DVD + CD

ADDITIONAL *AL-KITAAB* SERIES PRODUCTS

Al-Kitaab, Part One, Audio On the Go
ISBN 978-1-58901-150-2, CD

Al-Kitaab, Part Two, Audio On the Go
ISBN 978-1-58901-151-9, CD

Levantine Videos for *Al-Kitaab*: From *Alif Baa* to *Al-Kitaab, Part Three*
ISBN 978-1-58901-509-8, DVD

Available for iOS and Android in Fall 2015!

YALLAH
Learn Arabic with *Al-Kitaab*
The official study companion for *Alif Baa* and *Al-Kitaab*

YALLAH--developed from Flashcards Deluxe, one of the highest rated flashcard apps--is designed to be used either in conjunction with the *Al-Kitaab* Arabic Language textbook program or by independent students eager to master Arabic vocabulary. Students can choose to purchase Egyptian or Levantine spoken Arabic and will receive the corresponding MSA with it.

For price and ordering information, visit our website at
www.press.georgetown.edu/al-kitaab or call 800-537-5487.
For bulk purchases, contact the Georgetown University Press Marketing and
Sales Director at 202-687-9856.